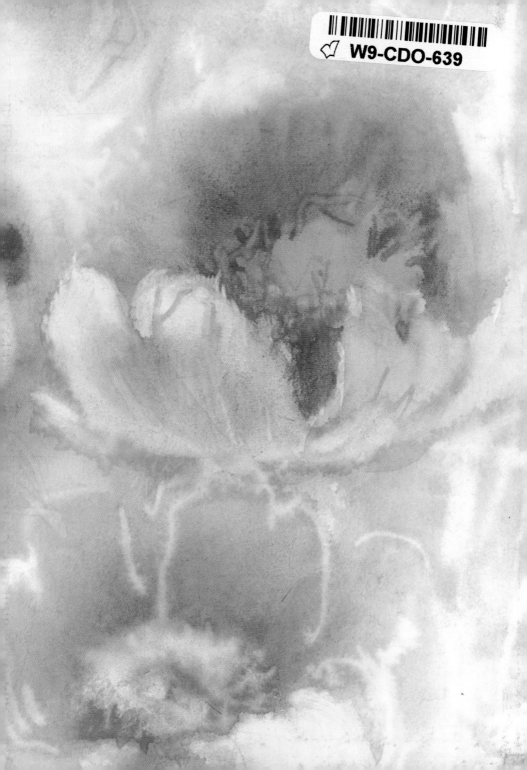

Presented to:

By:

Date:

Occasion:

NEVER LOSE HEART

THE POWER OF BEING POSITIVE

JOYCE MEYER

WARNER
Faith

New York • Boston • Nashville

NEVER LOSE HEART

CONTENTS

THE POWER OF
BEING POSITIVE

CONTENTS

NEVER LOSE
HEART

WHEN YOU FEEL STRESSED

*Peace comes to every situation
when we choose to listen to and obey
the Lord. We must follow Wisdom
to enjoy blessed lives.*

GOD'S WORD FOR YOU

Be anxious for nothing, but in everything by prayer and supplication with thanksgiving let your requests be made known to God.

And the peace of God, which surpasses all comprehension, will guard your hearts and your minds in Christ Jesus.

PHILIPPIANS 4:6-7 NASB

one

WHEN YOU FEEL STRESSED

 few years ago, I went to a doctor because I was constantly sick. He told me the symptoms were the result of being under stress. I was sleeping wrong, eating improperly, and pushing myself harder and harder—all in the name of working for the Lord.

The word *stress* was originally an engineering term used to refer to the amount of force that a beam or other physical support could bear without collapsing under the strain. In our time, stress has been expanded to include mental and emotional tension.

Stress is a normal part of everyone's life. God has created us to withstand a certain amount of pressure and tension. The problem comes when we push beyond our limitations and head toward doing permanent damage to ourselves.

Peace is meant to be the normal condition for every believer in Jesus Christ. He is the Prince of Peace, and in Jesus we find our own inheritance of peace. It is a gift from the Holy Spirit, which He gives as we live in obedience to His Word.

The peace Jesus gives operates in good times or bad,
when you are abounding or being abased.
His peace operates in the middle of a storm.

GOD'S WORD FOR YOU

Do you not know that your body is the temple (the very sanctuary) of the Holy Spirit Who lives within you, Whom you have received [as a Gift] from God? You are not your own,

You were bought with a price [purchased with a preciousness and paid for, made His own]. So then, honor God and bring glory to Him in your body.

1 CORINTHIANS 6:19-20

❧

Have you not known? Have you not heard? The everlasting God, the Lord, the Creator of the ends of the earth, does not faint or grow weary; there is no searching of His understanding.

He gives power to the faint and weary, and to him who has no might He increases strength [causing it to multiply and making it to abound].

ISAIAH 40:28-29

REFRESH THE WEARY

The first key to handling or overcoming stress is to recognize or admit we are under it. Though I was constantly having headaches, backaches, stomach-aches, neck aches, and all the other symptoms of stress, I found it very difficult to admit that I was pushing too hard physically, mentally, emotionally, and spiritually. I was doing the work I felt God wanted me to do without actually seeking Him to find out which work He wanted me to do, when He wanted me to do it, and how much of it. If we abuse ourselves, we will suffer the consequences.

Although the Lord gives power to the faint and weary, if you are worn out from continually exceeding your physical limitations, you need physical rest. The Lord may mercifully give you supernatural energy in particular instances, but you are in disobedience when you abuse your body, the temple of the Holy Spirit.

If you want God to flow and work through you, you need to take care of your body so God can use you. If you wear out your body, you don't have a spare in the drawer somewhere to pull out!

The anointing of God lifts when you operate outside of His promptings.

15

GOD'S WORD FOR YOU

*I, Wisdom [from God], make prudence my dwelling,
and I find out knowledge and discretion.*

PROVERBS 8:12

❧

*The Wisdom (godly Wisdom, which is comprehensive
insight into the ways and purposes of God] of the prudent
is to understand his way. . . .*

PROVERBS 14:8

❧

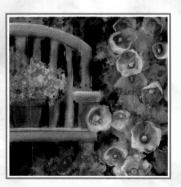

PRUDENCE

A word you don't hear very much teaching about is "prudence." In the Scriptures "prudence" or "prudent" means being good stewards of the gifts God has given us to use. Those gifts include time, energy, strength, and health as well as material possessions. They include our bodies as well as our minds and spirits.

Just as each one of us has been given a different set of gifts, each of us has been given a different ability to manage those gifts. Some of us are better able to manage ourselves than are others.

Each of us needs to know how much we are able to handle. We need to be able to recognize when we are reaching "full capacity" or "overload." Instead of pushing ourselves into overload to please others, satisfy our own desires, or reach our personal goals, we need to listen to the Lord and obey Him. We must follow Wisdom to enjoy blessed lives.

Nobody can remove all the stressors, the things causing or increasing stress, in our lives. For that reason, each of us must be *prudent* to identify and recognize the stressors that affect us most and learn how to respond to them with the right action.

God is good, and He wants you to believe
that He has a good plan for your life,
and that He is working in your situation.

17

GOD'S WORD FOR YOU

If you will listen diligently to the voice of the Lord your God, being watchful to do all His commandments which I command you this day, the Lord your God will set you high above all the nations of the earth.

And the Lord shall make you the head, and not the tail; and you shall be above only, and you shall not be beneath. . . .

DEUTERONOMY 28:1, 13

. . . now we serve not under [obedience to] the old code of written regulations, but [under obedience to the promptings] of the Spirit in newness [of life].

ROMANS 7:6

RELIEVING STRESS

When I began to prepare this message on stress, I asked the Lord to show me how He wanted me to present the material. The answer He gave me is a message, a word, from the heart of the Father for the Body of Christ for this hour, this season.

Another important key to relieving stress is *obedience*.

We may have stress, but we will be on *top* of it, not *under* it. There is a big difference between being *under* stress and being on *top* of a situation!

All of us have situations that come our way we don't like. But, with the power of God, we can go through those circumstances stress free.

Even though, like the people in the world, we will sometimes experience stressful times, if we are obedient to God's Word and to His promptings, we can be on top of stress and not under it.

Do you believe that God is leading you into a place of victory and triumph, not into a place of defeat? Your answer as a child of God and believer in Jesus Christ would be yes! If we believers would listen to everything the Lord tells us and obey Him, we would not get into that state of defeat so often.

Simply obeying the promptings of the Holy Spirit will often relieve stress quickly.

GOD'S WORD FOR YOU

Do you not know that if you continually surrender yourselves to anyone to do his will, you are the slaves of him whom you obey, whether that be to sin, which leads to death, or to obedience which leads to righteousness (right doing and right standing with God)?

ROMANS 6:16

Now therefore, if you will obey My voice in truth and keep My covenant, then you shall be My own peculiar possession and treasure from among and above all peoples; for all the earth is Mine.

EXODUS 19:5

GOD'S ANOINTING IS ON OBEDIENCE

God's grace and power are available for us to use. God enables us or gives us an anointing of the Holy Spirit to do what *He* tells us to do. Sometimes after He has prompted us to go another direction, we still keep pressing on with our original plan. If we are doing something He has not approved, He is under no obligation to give us the energy to do it. We are functioning in our own strength rather than under the control of the Holy Spirit. Then we get so frustrated, stressed, or burned out, we lose our self-control, simply by ignoring the promptings of the Spirit.

Many people are stressed and burned out from going their own way instead of God's way. They end up in stressful situations when they go a different direction from the one God prompted. Then they burn out in the midst of the disobedience and, struggling to finish what they started outside of God's direction, beg God to anoint them.

God is merciful, and He helps us in the midst of our mistakes. But He is not going to give us strength and energy to disobey Him continually. We can avoid many stressful situations and living "tied up in knots" simply by obeying the Holy Spirit's promptings moment by moment.

Obeying Him in the little things makes a major difference in keeping stress out of our life.

GOD'S WORD FOR YOU

Let be and be still, and know (recognize and understand) that I am God. I will be exalted among the nations! I will be exalted in the earth!

PSALM 46:10

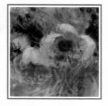

Lean on, trust in, and be confident in the Lord with all your heart and mind and do not rely on your own insight or understanding.

In all your ways know, recognize, and acknowledge Him, and He will direct and make straight and plain your paths.

PROVERBS 3:5-6

BE STILL AND KNOW GOD

One of the main reasons so many of us are burned out and stressed out is that we don't know how to be still, to "know" God and "acknowledge" Him. When we spend time with Him, we learn to hear His voice. When we acknowledge Him, He directs our paths. We need to learn to be quiet inside and stay in that peaceful state so that we are always ready to hear the Lord's voice.

Many people today run from one thing to the next. Because their minds don't know how to be still, they don't know how to be still.

For a long time I felt I had to find something to do every evening. I had to be involved and a part of whatever was going on. I thought I couldn't afford to miss anything because I didn't want anything to go on that I didn't know about. I couldn't just sit and be still. I had to be up doing something. I was not a human being—I was a human doing.

We need to be careful to submit our ideas and plans to God, then slow down and wait. Make sure there is a sense of peace to go along with the plans and ideas. Ask the Lord for His will in your life, then be still and know that He is God.

God gives His highest and best to those whose trust is in Him. Be still and let Him show Himself strong in your life.

GOD'S WORD FOR YOU

Peace I leave with you; My [own] peace I now give and bequeath to you. Not as the world gives do I give to you. Do not let your hearts be troubled, neither let them be afraid. [Stop allowing yourselves to be agitated and disturbed; and do not permit yourselves to be fearful and intimidated and cowardly and unsettled.]

JOHN 14:27

And let the peace (soul harmony which comes) from Christ rule (act as umpire continually) in your hearts [deciding and settling with finality all questions that arise in your minds, in that peaceful state].

COLOSSIANS 3:15

JESUS, OUR PRINCE OF PEACE

When we are all stressed out, we would like to eliminate the causes of the problems, but the source of stress is not really difficulties, circumstances, and situations. Stress comes from approaching problems with the world's perspective rather than faith in Jesus Christ, the Prince of Peace.

It was Jesus' blood that bought our peace, but the price we must pay for peace is a willingness to change our approach to life. We will never enjoy peace without a willingness to adjust and adapt ourselves. We must be willing to sacrifice worry and reasoning if we are to know peace. We cannot have anxiety, frustration, or rigid, legalistic attitudes and enjoy the peace of God.

Even though we will have disturbing issues to deal with, we can have Jesus' peace because He has "overcome the world" and "deprived" the world of its "power to harm" us. He left us with the power to "stop allowing" ourselves "to be agitated and disturbed"! Peace is available, but we must choose it!

The Prince of Peace, Jesus, Who lives inside those of us who have received Him, knows and will reveal to us the specific actions we need to take in every situation to lead us into peace.

It is absolutely amazing what we can accomplish in Christ if we live one day at a time in His peace.

GOD'S WORD FOR YOU

Even when we were dead (slain) by [our own]
shortcomings and trespasses, He made us alive together in
fellowship and in union with Christ; [He gave us the very
life of Christ Himself, the same new life with which He
quickened Him, for] it is by grace (His favor and mercy
which you did not deserve) that you are saved (delivered
from judgment and made partakers of Christ's salvation).

EPHESIANS 2:5

But He gives us more and more grace (power of the
Holy Spirit, to meet this evil tendency and all others fully).
. . . God sets Himself against the proud . . . but gives
grace [continually] to the lowly (those who are humble
enough to receive it).

JAMES 4:6

WORKS VERSUS GRACE

We get so frustrated because we are trying to live by *works* a life that was brought into being and designed by God to be lived by *grace*. The more we try to figure out what to do to solve our dilemma, the more confused, upset, and frustrated we become.

When you get into a frustrating situation, just stop and say, "O Lord, give me grace." Then believe that God has heard your prayer and is answering that prayer and working out that situation.

Faith is the channel through which you and I receive the grace of God. If we try to do things on our own without being open to receive the grace of God, then no matter how much faith we may have, we will still not receive what we are asking of God.

A long time ago I wrote up this statement and stuck it on my refrigerator:

Works of the flesh = Frustration.

If you can learn this principle, you will soon overcome the evil tendency to become frustrated.

We need to trust in and rely on the grace of God. He knows what we are facing in every situation of life, and He will work out things for the best if we will trust Him enough to allow Him to do so.

❦

Remember, it is not by power or by might, but by the Spirit that we win the victory over our enemy.

GOD'S WORD FOR YOU

Now unto him that is able to do exceeding abundantly above all that we ask or think, according to the power that worketh in us.

EPHESIANS 3:20 KJV

GOD IS ABLE

This is a powerful Scripture that tells us that our God is able—able to do far above and beyond anything that you and I can ever dare to hope, ask, or even think. We need to pray, to do the asking in faith and in trust. But it is God Who does the work, not us. How does He do it? *According to* [or by] *the power* [or grace of God] *that worketh in us*. Whatever you and I receive from the Lord is directly related to the amount of grace we learn to receive.

I was putting unbelievable stress on myself trying to change. I was under tremendous condemnation because every message I heard seemed to be telling me to change, yet I couldn't change no matter how hard I tried, believed, or confessed. I was in a terrible mess because I saw all the things about me that needed to be changed, but I was powerless to bring about those changes.

The Lord has to be our Source and our Supply. He is the only One who can bring about changes in our lives. I had to learn to say, "Father, although I am not worthy of Your help, I know that the changes You want in my life are not going to work unless You add the power."

*God promises to strengthen us in our weaknesses
if we trust Him and turn to Him. God's grace
will be sufficient in our need.*

When You Feel Discouraged

Happiness and joy do not come from the outside. They come from within. They are a conscious decision, a deliberate choice, one that we make ourselves each day we live.

GOD'S WORD FOR YOU

[What, what would have become of me] had I not believed that I would see the Lord's goodness in the land of the living!

Wait and hope for and expect the Lord; be brave and of good courage and let your heart be stout and enduring. Yes, wait for and hope for and expect the Lord.

PSALM 27:13-14

For I know the thoughts and plans that I have for you, says the Lord, thoughts and plans for welfare and peace and not for evil, to give you hope in your final outcome.

JEREMIAH 29:11

t w o

WHEN YOU FEEL DISCOURAGED

We have all been disappointed at some time. It would be surprising if we went through the week without encountering some kind of disappointment. We are "appointed" (set in a certain direction) for something to happen a certain way, and when it doesn't happen that way, we become "dis-appointed."

Disappointment not dealt with turns into discouragement. If we stay discouraged very long, we are liable to become devastated, and devastation leaves us unable to handle anything.

Many devastated Christians are lying along the roadside of life because they have not learned how to handle disappointment. The devastation they are experiencing now most likely began with a minor disappointment that was not dealt with properly.

It is not God's will for us to live disappointed, devastated, or oppressed! When we become "disappointed," we must learn to become "re-appointed" to keep from becoming discouraged, then devastated.

When we learn to place our hope and confidence in Jesus the Rock (1 Corinthians 10:4) and resist the devil at the onset, we can live in the joy and peace of the Lord, free from discouragement.

Choose to aggressively withstand the devil so you can live in the fullness of life God has provided for you through His Son Jesus Christ.

GOD'S WORD FOR YOU

. . . for God selected (deliberately chose) what in the world is foolish to put the wise to shame, and what the world calls weak to put the strong to shame.

And God also selected (deliberately chose) what in the world is lowborn and insignificant and branded and treated with contempt, even the things that are nothing, that He might depose and bring to nothing the things that are,

So that no mortal man should [have pretense for glorying and] boast in the presence of God.

1 CORINTHIANS 1:27-29

GOD CHOOSES THE UNLIKELY

When you feel discouraged, remember that God chose you for His very own purpose, however unlikely a candidate you feel. By doing so, He has placed before you a wide open door to show you His boundless grace, mercy, and power to change your life.

When God uses any one of us, though we may all feel inadequate and unworthy, we realize that our source is not in ourselves but in Him alone: "[This is] because the foolish thing [that has its source in] God is wiser than men, and the weak thing [that springs] from God is stronger than men" (1 Corinthians 1:25).

Each of us has a destiny, and there is absolutely no excuse not to fulfill it. We cannot use our weakness as an excuse because God says that His strength is made perfect in weakness (2 Corinthians 12:9). We cannot use the past as an excuse because God tells us through the apostle Paul that if any person is in Christ, he is a new creature; old things have passed away, and all things have become new (2 Corinthians 5:17).

Spend some time with yourself and take an inventory of how you feel about yourself. What is your image of yourself? Do you see yourself re-created in God's image, resurrected to a brand-new life that is just waiting for you to claim it?

Each of us can succeed at being
everything God intends us to be.

GOD'S WORD FOR YOU

. . . the Word of God . . . is effectually at work in you who believe [exercising its superhuman power in those who adhere to and trust in and rely on it].

1 THESSALONIANS 2:13

WE ARE A "WORK IN PROGRESS"

I encourage you to say every day, "*God is working in me right now—He is changing me!*" Speak out of your mouth what the Word says, not what you feel. When we incessantly talk about how we feel, it is difficult for the Word of God to work in us effectively.

As we step out to be all we can be in Christ, we will make some mistakes—everyone does. But it takes the pressure off of us when we realize that God is expecting us to do the best we can. He is not expecting us to be perfect (totally without flaw). If we were as perfect as we try to be, we would not need a Savior. I believe God will always leave a certain number of defects in us, just so we will know how much we need Jesus every single day.

I am not a perfect preacher. There are times when I say things wrong, times when I believe I have heard from God and find out I was hearing from myself. There are many times when I fall short of perfection. I don't have perfect faith, a perfect attitude, perfect thoughts, and perfect ways.

Jesus knew that would happen to all of us. That is why He stands in the gap between God's perfection and our imperfection. He *continually* intercedes for us because we *continually* need it (Hebrews 7:25).

We do not have to believe that God accepts us only if we perform perfectly. We can believe the truth that He accepts us "in the Beloved."

GOD'S WORD FOR YOU

Fight the good fight of the faith; lay hold of the eternal life to which you were summoned and [for which] you confessed the good confession [of faith] before many witnesses.

1 TIMOTHY 6:12

BE A FIGHTER

To be aggressive is to be a fighter. Just as the apostle Paul said that he had fought the good fight of faith (2 Timothy 4:7), so he instructed his young disciple Timothy to fight the good fight of faith. In the same way, we are to fight the good fight of faith in our daily lives as we struggle against spiritual enemies in high places and in our own mind and heart.

One part of fighting the good fight of faith is being able to recognize the enemy. As long as we are passive, Satan will torment us. Nothing is going to change about our situation if all we do is just sit and wish things were different. We have to take action. Too often we don't move against the enemy when he comes against us with discouragement or fear or doubt or guilt. We just draw back into a corner somewhere and let him beat us up.

You and I are not supposed to be punching bags for the devil; instead, we are supposed to be fighters.

Now the devil wants us to fight in the natural with everybody around us. But God wants us to forget all the junk that Satan stirs up within us to get us riled up against other people. Instead, He wants us to fight against the spiritual enemies who try to war over our lives and steal our peace and joy.

Come against Satan when he is trying to get a foothold, and he will never get a stronghold.

GOD'S WORD FOR YOU

For as many as are the promises of God, they all find their Yes [answer] in Him [Christ]. For this reason we also utter the Amen (so be it) to God through Him [in His Person and by His agency] to the glory of God.

2 CORINTHIANS 1:20

CONFIDENCE IN JESUS

In several places in the Bible, for example in
1 Corinthians 10:4, Jesus is referred to as the Rock.
The apostle Paul goes on to tell us in Colossians 2:7
that we are to be rooted and grounded in Him.

If we get our roots wrapped around Jesus Christ, we
are in good shape. But if we get them wrapped around
anything or anyone else, we are in trouble.

Nothing nor no one is going to be as solid and
dependable and immovable as Jesus. That's why I don't
want people to get rooted and grounded in me or my
ministry. I want to point people to Jesus. I know that
ultimately I will fail them in some way, just as I know
they will ultimately fail me.

That's the problem with us humans; we are always
liable to failure. But Jesus Christ isn't. Put your hope
wholly and unchangeably in Him. Not in man, not in
circumstances, not in anything or anyone else.

If you don't put your hope and faith in the Rock of
your salvation, you are headed for disappointment,
which leads to discouragement and devastation. We
should have so much confidence in God's love for us
that no matter what comes against us, we know deep
inside that we are more than conquerors.

❧

*We need to come to a state of utter bankruptcy in our
own ability apart from Christ. Without God, we are
helpless; with Him nothing is impossible to us.*

41

GOD'S WORD FOR YOU

. . . let us run with patient endurance and steady and active persistence the appointed course of the race that is set before us.

Looking away [from all that will distract] to Jesus, Who is the Leader and the Source of our faith [giving the first incentive for our belief] and is also its Finisher [bringing it to maturity and perfection]. He, for the joy [of obtaining the prize] that was set before Him, endured the cross, despising and ignoring the shame, and is now seated at the right hand of the throne of God.

Just think of Him Who endured from sinners such grievous opposition and bitter hostility against Himself [reckon up and consider it all in comparison with your trials], so that you may not grow weary or exhausted, losing heart and relaxing and fainting in your minds.

HEBREWS 12:1-3

Keep On Looking to Jesus

It does not take any special talent to give up and lie down on the side of the road of life and say, "I quit." Any unbeliever can do that.

You don't have to be a Christian to be a quitter. But once you get hold of Jesus, or better yet when He gets hold of you, He begins to pump strength and energy and courage into you, and something strange and wonderful begins to happen. He won't let you quit!

I used to want to give up and quit. But now I get out of bed and start each day afresh and anew. I begin my day by praying and reading the Bible and speaking the Word, seeking after God.

The devil may be screaming in my ear, "That's not doing you one bit of good. You've been doing that for years and look what it's got you—you still have trouble."

That's when I say, "Shut up, devil! The Bible says that I am to look to Jesus and follow His example. He is my Leader, the Source and Finisher of my faith.

You and I need to make a decision today that, come what may, we are going to keep pressing on, looking to Jesus, no matter what.

GOD'S WORD FOR YOU

Do not fret or have any anxiety about anything, but in every circumstance and in everything, by prayer and petition (definite requests), with thanksgiving, continue to make your wants known to God.

And God's peace [shall be yours, that tranquil state of a soul assured of its salvation through Christ, and so fearing nothing from God and being content with its earthly lot of whatever sort that is, that peace] which transcends all understanding shall garrison and mount guard over your hearts and minds in Christ Jesus.

PHILIPPIANS 4:6-7

MEDITATE ON THE THINGS OF GOD

If you don't want to be devastated by discouragement, then don't meditate on your disappointments.

Did you know that your feelings are hooked up to your thinking? If you don't think that is true, just take about twenty minutes or so and think about nothing but your problems. I can assure you that by the end of that time your feelings and maybe even your countenance will have changed.

I got up one day thinking about a problem I had. Suddenly the Spirit of the Lord spoke to me. He said to me, "Joyce, are you going to fellowship with your problem or with Me?"

When you get disappointed, don't sit around and feel sorry for yourself. As bad as things may seem, we still have a choice. We can choose to fellowship with our problems or fellowship with God.

We can allow our thoughts to dwell on the bad things until we become totally discouraged and devastated, or we can focus our attention on all the good things that have happened to us in our life—and on all the blessings that God still has in store for us in the days ahead.

Our thoughts are silent words that only we and the Lord hear, but those words affect our inner man, our health, our joy, and our attitude.

GOD'S WORD FOR YOU

Catch the foxes for us, the little foxes that are ruining the vineyards. . . .

SONG OF SOLOMON 2:15 NASB

CATCH THE FOXES

Little disappointments can create frustration, which in turn may lead to bigger problems that can produce a great deal of damage.

Besides the huge disappointments that occur when we fail to get the job promotion or house we wanted, we can become just as upset by minor annoyances. For example, suppose someone is supposed to meet you for lunch and fails to show up. Or suppose you make a special trip to the mall to buy something at a discount, but it's all sold out.

All these kinds of frustrations are actually minor, but they can add up to cause a lot of grief. That's why we have to know how to handle them and keep them in perspective. Otherwise, they can get out of hand and be blown up all out of proportion.

We have to be on our guard against the little foxes that destroy the vineyards, because all together they can do just as much damage as the serious disappointments that often accompany them.

We must learn to do as Paul did in the book of Acts when the serpent attached itself to his hand—he simply shook it off (Acts 28:1-5)! If we practice dealing quickly with disappointments as they come, they will not pile up into a mountain of devastation.

Victory is not the absence of problems;
it is the presence of God's power.

GOD'S WORD FOR YOU

The mystery of which was hidden for ages and generations [from angels and men], but is now revealed to His holy people (the saints),

To whom God was pleased to make known how great for the Gentiles are the riches of the glory of this mystery, which is Christ within and among you, the Hope of [realizing the] glory.

COLOSSIANS 1:26-27

CHRIST IN YOU, THE HOPE OF GLORY

You and I can only realize and experience the glory of God on our lives because of Christ in us. He is our hope of seeing better things.

The glory of God is His manifested excellence. As the children of God, we have a blood-bought right to experience the best God has planned for us. Satan furiously fights the plan of God in each of our lives, and his primary weapon is deception. When we are deceived, we believe something that is not true.

When we look at ourselves and our own ability, we feel defeated, but remembering that Christ lives in us is our hope of realizing the glory. It keeps us encouraged enough to press on toward better things. We limit ourselves when we look to ourselves alone and fail to see Jesus.

The Lord has destined His Church for glory. He is coming back for a glorious Church (Ephesians 5:27). God's glory can be manifested in us and on us, but only as we believe it is possible.

God is looking for someone who will believe and receive. He is waiting to manifest His glory —to you and through you!

WHEN
YOU FEEL
WORRIED

God has a secret place
of abiding where worry
vanishes and peace reigns.

GOD'S WORD FOR YOU

Humble yourselves therefore under the mighty hand of God, that he may exalt you in due time:
Casting all your care upon him; for he careth for you.

1 PETER 5:6-7 KJV

The Spirit of the Lord God is upon me, because the Lord has anointed and qualified me. . . . To grant [consolation and joy] to those who mourn in Zion—to give them an ornament (a garland or diadem) of beauty instead of ashes ["beauty for ashes" KJV].

ISAIAH 61:1, 3

three

WHEN YOU FEEL WORRIED

od wants to take care of us, but in order to let Him, *we* must stop taking the care. Many people want God to take care of them while they are worrying or trying to figure out an answer instead of waiting for God's direction. They are actually wallowing around in their "ashes," but they still want God to give them beauty. In order for God to give us the beauty, we must give Him the "ashes."

We give Him our cares by trusting that He can and will take care of us. Hebrews 4:3 says: "For we who have believed (adhered to and trusted in and relied on God) do enter that rest. . . ."

We enter into the Lord's rest through believing. Worry is the opposite of faith. Worry steals our peace, physically wears us out, and can even make us sick. If we are worrying, we are not trusting God, and we are not entering God's rest.

What a great trade! You give God ashes, and He gives you beauty. You give Him all your worries and concerns, and He gives you protection, stability, a place of refuge and fullness of joy—the privilege of being cared for by Him.

*Jesus did not worry,
and we do not have to worry either.*

GOD'S WORD FOR YOU

He who dwells in the secret place of the Most High shall remain stable and fixed under the shadow of the Almighty [Whose power no foe can withstand].

PSALM 91:1

*A*BIDING IN PROTECTION

God has a secret place where we can dwell in peace and safety.

The secret place is the place of rest in God, a place of peace and comfort in Him. This secret place is a "spiritual place" where worry vanishes and peace reigns. It is the place of God's presence. When we spend time praying and seeking God and dwelling in His presence, we are in the secret place.

When you and I *dwell in Christ* or *dwell in the secret place*, we do not just visit there occasionally, we take up permanent residence there.

The secret place is a hiding place, a private place, or a place of refuge. It is the place we run to when we are hurting, overwhelmed, or feeling faint. It is the place we run to when we are being mistreated or persecuted, when we are in great need, or when we feel we just cannot take it anymore.

We need to be firmly planted in God. We need to know the Source of our help in every situation and in every circumstance. We need to have our own secret place of peace and security. We need to rely on God and trust Him completely.

God wants us to take refuge under the protective shadow of His wings. He wants us to run to Him!

GOD'S WORD FOR YOU

Therefore do not worry and be anxious, saying, What are we going to have to eat? or, What are we going to have to drink? or, What are we going to have to wear?

For the Gentiles (heathen) wish for and crave and diligently seek all these things, and your heavenly Father knows well that you need them all.

MATTHEW 6:31-32

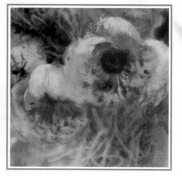

_DON'T BE ANXIOUS

The problem with worry is that it causes us to start saying: "What are we going to have to eat? What are we going to have to drink? What are we going to have to wear?" In other words, "What are we going to do if God doesn't come through for us?"

Instead of calming our fears and removing our worries, we begin to fret and fuss with the words of our mouth, which only makes them even more deeply ingrained.

The problem with this way of doing things is that it is the way people act who don't know they have a heavenly Father. But you and I do know we have a heavenly Father, so we need to act like it.

Jesus assures us that our heavenly Father knows all our needs before we ask Him. So why should we worry about them? Instead, we need to focus our attention on the things that are much more important—the things of God.

❧

Seek first the Kingdom of God
and His righteousness; then all these
other things we need will be added to us.

GOD'S WORD FOR YOU

Only it must be in faith that he asks with no wavering (no hesitating, no doubting). For the one who wavers (hesitates, doubts) is like the billowing surge out at sea that is blown hither and thither and tossed by the wind.

For truly, let not such a person imagine that he will receive anything [he asks for] from the Lord.

JAMES 1:6-7

STAY IN THE POSITIVE

If we take our concerns to the Lord in prayer and then continue to worry about them, we are mixing a positive and a negative force. Prayer is a positive force, and worry is a negative force. If we add them together, we come up with zero. I don't know about you, but I don't want to have zero power, so I try not to mix prayer and worry.

God spoke to me one time and said, "Many people operate with zero power because they are always mixing the positives and the negatives. They have a positive confession for a little while, then a negative confession for a little while. They pray for a little while, then they worry for a little while. They trust for a little while, then they worry for a little while. As a result, they just go back and forth, never really making any progress."

Let's not magnify the bad—let's magnify the good! Let's make it larger by talking about it, by being positive in our thoughts, in our attitudes, in our outlook, in our words, and in our actions.

Why not make a decision to stay in the positive by trusting God and refusing to worry?

Practice being positive in each situation that arises. Even if whatever is taking place at the moment is not so good, expect God to bring good out of it.

GOD'S WORD FOR YOU

*Let the redeemed of the Lord say so, whom He has
delivered from the hand of the adversary.*

PSALM 107:2

*For [then] He will deliver you from the snare of the
fowler and from the deadly pestilence.
[Then] He will cover you with His pinions, and under
His wings shall you trust and find refuge; His truth and
His faithfulness are a shield and a buckler.*

PSALM 91:3-4

IF YOU'RE REDEEMED, SAY SO!

When you realize that the devil is trying to distract you, don't just sit around and let him beat you up with worry and negative thoughts. Open your mouth and begin to confess your authority in Christ.

Sometimes while I am preparing to speak at a church or seminar, negative thoughts will begin to bombard me. At those times I encourage myself with my own mouth and say out loud, "Everything is going to be all right."

Satan places anxious and worried thoughts in our minds, sometimes actually "bombarding" our minds with them. He hopes we will receive them and begin "saying" them out of our mouths. If we do, he then has material to actually create the circumstances in our lives he has been giving us anxious thoughts about.

Once I recognized those anxious thoughts and evil forebodings and took authority over them, God began to bring some deliverance to my life so I could start to enjoy it.

Don't be the devil's mouthpiece.

Find out what God's Word promises you and begin to declare His two-edged sword (Hebrews 4:12).

*As we speak the Word out of our mouths
in faith, we wield a mighty two-edged sword
that destroys the enemy.*

GOD'S WORD FOR YOU

Beloved, we are [even here and] now God's children; it is not yet disclosed (made clear) what we shall be [hereafter], but we know that when He comes and is manifested, we shall [as God's children] resemble and be like Him, for we shall see Him just as He [really] is.

1 JOHN 3:2

LIVE IN THE NOW

In reality, the choices we make today will determine whether we will enjoy the moment or waste it by worrying. Sometimes we end up missing the moment of today because we are too concerned about tomorrow. We need to keep our mind focused on what God wants us to be doing now.

God gave me a definition of anxiety: "Anxiety is caused by trying to mentally or emotionally get into things that are not here yet (the future) or things that have already been (the past)."

One of the things that we need to understand is that God wants us to learn how to be *now* people. For example, 2 Corinthians 6:2 KJV says, "Behold, now is the day of salvation," and Hebrews 4:7 says, "Today, if you would hear His voice and when you hear it, do not harden your hearts."

We need to learn to live now. Often we spend our mental time in the past or the future. When we don't really give ourselves to what we are doing at the moment, we become prone to anxiety. If we will live in the now, we will find the Lord there with us. Regardless of what situations life brings our way, He has promised never to leave us or forsake us but to always be with us and help us (Hebrews 13:5; Matthew 28:20).

*Don't waste your precious "now"
worrying about yesterday or tomorrow.*

GOD'S WORD FOR YOU

But be doers of the Word [obey the message], and not merely listeners to it, betraying yourselves [into deception by reasoning contrary to the Truth].

JAMES 1:22

GIVE UP EXCESSIVE REASONING

Are you always trying to figure everything out? Many of us have fallen into that ditch. Instead of casting our care upon the Lord, we go through life carrying every bit of it.

When we try to figure everything out, we are exalting our reasoning above God's thoughts. We are placing our ways higher than His ways. When God revealed to me that I had to give up excessive reasoning that was contrary to the truth, it was a real challenge. I couldn't stand it if I did not have everything figured out.

For example, God told us to do some things in our ministry several years ago that I didn't have the slightest idea how to go about doing. But God never called me to figure out exactly how to accomplish everything He asked me to do. He called me to seek *Him* rather than the answer to my problems, then obey what He told me to do.

When we worry, we lose our peace, and when we try to figure everything out, we fall into confusion. Confusion is the result of reasoning with our own understanding when we should be trusting in the Lord with all our heart to make the way for us according to His plan. When we trust that His thoughts are higher than our thoughts, we stop confusion before it starts.

God's peace is always available,
but we must choose it.

GOD'S WORD FOR YOU

So trust in the Lord (commit yourself to Him, lean on Him, hope confidently in Him) forever; for the Lord God is an everlasting Rock [the Rock of Ages].

ISAIAH 26:4

O my God, I trust, lean on, rely on, and am confident in You.

PSALM 25:2

DEVELOPING TRUST

How many times have you frustrated yourself and gotten all upset needlessly over trying situations that came your way? How many years of your life have you spent saying, "Oh, I'm believing God. I'm trusting God," when, in reality, all you were doing was worrying, talking negatively, and trying to figure out everything on your own? You may have thought you were trusting God because you were saying, "I trust God," but inside you were anxious and panicky. You were trying to learn to trust God, but you were not quite there yet.

Trust and confidence are built up over a period of time. It usually takes some time to overcome an ingrained habit of worry, anxiety, or fear. That is why it is so important to "hang in there" with God. Don't quit and give up, because you gain experience and spiritual strength every round you go through. Each time you become a little stronger than you were the last time. Sooner or later, if you don't give up, you will be more than the devil can handle.

If you are in a time of trials, use that time to build your trust in God. Trust Him to deliver you or bring you through successfully.

GOD'S WORD FOR YOU

Be well balanced. . . .

1 PETER 5:8

You will guard him and keep him in perfect and constant peace whose mind [both its inclination and its character] is stayed on You, because he commits himself to You, leans on You, and hopes confidently in You.

ISAIAH 26:3

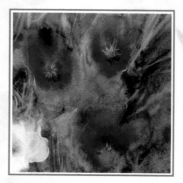

BE WELL-BALANCED

Sometimes in trying situations our anxiety gets in the way of our doing what we should. All we can do is our best, then trust God with the rest.

We function best when we have a calm, well-balanced mind. When our mind is calm, it is without fear, worry, or torment. When our mind is well-balanced, we are able to look the situation over and decide what to do or not to do about it.

Where most of us get in trouble is when we get out of balance. Either we move into a state of total passivity in which we do nothing, expecting God to do everything for us, or we become hyperactive, operating most of the time in the flesh. God wants us to be well-balanced so that we are able to face any situation of life and say, "Well, I believe I can do certain things about this situation, but no more."

Instead of getting distraught and full of fear and worry, we need to go before God and say, "Well, Lord, I'm believing You to help me in this situation, but is there something You want me to do?"

Whatever it is that God shows us to do about our problem, we need to be diligent enough to do it. Then we need to trust Him with the outcome.

Once we have done all we know to do,
we can trust God with the rest.
That is what I call faith and balance.

WHEN YOU FEEL INSECURE

God is looking for people with
a right heart attitude toward Him,
not a perfect performance record.

GOD'S WORD FOR YOU

May you be rooted deep in love and founded securely on love,

That you may have the power and be strong to apprehend and grasp with all the saints [God's devoted people, the experience of that love] what is the breadth and length and height and depth [of it];

[That you may really come] to know [practically, through experience for yourselves] the love of Christ, which far surpasses mere knowledge [without experience]; that you may be filled [through all your being] unto all the fullness of God [may have the richest measure of the divine Presence, and become a body wholly filled and flooded with God Himself]!

EPHESIANS 3:17-19

four

WHEN YOU FEEL INSECURE

any people have a deep feeling of insecurity about themselves because they can't accept themselves for who they are. Are you tired of playing games, wearing masks, trying to be someone other than who you are? Wouldn't you like the freedom just to be accepted as you are, without pressure to be someone you really don't know how to be?

God wants us to learn our value is not in what we do but in who we are in Him. He wants us to be willing to be who we are, weaknesses and all, because He accepts us unconditionally.

The devil's plan is to deceive us into basing our worth on our performance, then keep us focused on all our faults and shortcomings. Satan wants us to have a low opinion of ourselves so that we live ineffectively for God, being miserable and unreceptive to God's blessings because we don't think we deserve them.

It is so important to have a positive sense of self-esteem, self-value, and self-worth, to be secure in who we are in Christ, to truly like ourselves. We learn to like ourselves by learning how much God loves us. Once we become rooted and grounded in God's love, we can come to terms of peace with ourselves and stop feeling insecure.

Every one of us is imperfect,
and God loves us just the way we are.

GOD'S WORD FOR YOU

That the communication of thy faith may become effectual by the acknowledging of every good thing which is in you in Christ Jesus.

PHILEMON 1:6 KJV

For by your words you will be justified and acquitted, and by your words you will be condemned and sentenced.

MATTHEW 12:37

ELIMINATE THE NEGATIVE

If we speak badly about ourselves, we will feel condemned. Let's apply what Jesus taught about our words as the first key to overcoming insecurity *and never speak negatively about ourselves*. We must speak words that empower us—not words that weaken us. If we want to increase our self-acceptance and our opinion of ourselves, we must decide that not one more negative comment about ourselves will ever come out of our mouth.

The devil wants us to acknowledge every bad trait we see in ourselves because he doesn't want the communication of our faith to be effectual. As the accuser of the brethren (Revelation 12:9-10), he continually tries to redirect our focus from who we are in Christ back on to our shortcomings.

We need to understand who we are in Christ and see how much He has done for us through shedding His blood to make us worthy. The communication of our faith is made effectual by acknowledging every *good thing* in us *in Christ Jesus*, not by acknowledging every *wrong thing* with *us*. Acts 10:15 says: "What God has cleansed and pronounced clean, do not you defile and profane by regarding and calling common and unhallowed or unclean."

Jesus was made perfect for us. Our acceptability to God is not based on our performance, but on our faith and trust in Jesus' performance.

GOD'S WORD FOR YOU

[Righteousness, standing acceptable to God] will be granted and credited to us also who believe in (trust in, adhere to, and rely on) God, Who raised Jesus our Lord from the dead.

ROMANS 4:24

For our sake He made Christ [virtually] to be sin Who knew no sin, so that in and through Him we might become [endued with, viewed as being in, and examples of] the righteousness of God [what we ought to be, approved and acceptable and in right relationship with Him, by His goodness].

2 CORINTHIANS 5:21

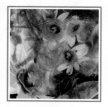

Righteousness Is God's Gift

One of the first revelations God gave me out of the Word was on righteousness. By "revelation" I mean one day you suddenly understand something to the point that it becomes part of you. The knowledge isn't only in your mind—you no longer need to renew your mind to it because you don't wonder or hope it's true—you *know*.

Righteousness is God's gift to us. It is "imputed"— granted and credited—to us by virtue of our believing in what God did for us through His Son Jesus Christ. Jesus, Who knew no sin, became sin so that we might be made the righteousness of God in Jesus.

Above all else, the devil does not want us to walk in the reality that we are in right standing with God. He wants us to feel insecure, always vaguely contemplating what is wrong with us.

Jesus wants us to know that we are right with God because of what He has done for us. He wants us to live in His Kingdom and have peace and joy in the midst of every tribulation.

When we keep our eyes on the true Kingdom of God—on Him, His righteousness, His peace, and His joy—the rest will be added to us in abundance.

GOD'S WORD FOR YOU

For we all often stumble and fall and offend in many things. And if anyone does not offend in speech [never says the wrong things], he is a fully developed character and a perfect man, able to control his whole body and to curb his entire nature.

JAMES 3:2

Death and life are in the power of the tongue, and they who indulge in it shall eat the fruit of it [for death or life]. [Matt. 12:37.]

PROVERBS 18:21

CELEBRATE THE POSITIVE

A key to overcoming insecurity is this: *Meditate on and speak positive things about yourself.*

Our thoughts and words about ourselves are tremendously important. In order to overcome the negative thinking and speaking that have been such a natural part of our lifestyle for so long, we must make a conscious effort to think and speak good things about ourselves to ourselves by making positive confessions.

We need to get our mouth in line with what the Word of God says about us. Positive confession of the Word of God should be an ingrained habit of every believer. If you have not yet begun to develop this important habit, start today. Begin thinking and saying good things about yourself: "I am the righteousness of God in Jesus Christ. I prosper in everything I lay my hand to. I have gifts and talents, and God is using me. I operate in the fruit of the Spirit. I walk in love. Joy flows through me."

The Bible teaches we can appropriate the blessings of God in our lives by believing and confessing the positive things God has said about us in His Word.

If you will continually and purposefully speak about yourself what the Word of God says about you, you will receive positive results.

GOD'S WORD FOR YOU

He said this to indicate by what kind of death Peter would glorify God. And after this, He said to him, Follow Me!

But Peter turned and saw the disciple whom Jesus loved, following—the one who also had leaned back on His breast at the supper and had said, Lord, who is it that is going to betray You?

When Peter saw him, he said to Jesus, Lord, what about this man?

JOHN 21:19-21

*A*VOID COMPARISONS

The next important key to overcoming insecurity is simple: *Never compare yourself with anyone else because it invites condemnation.*

I really want to encourage you to stop comparing yourself with other people about how you look, what position you occupy, or how long you pray. Comparison only thwarts God's working in your life.

We also must not compare our trials and tribulations to those of other people. Some situations may seem hard to you. But you cannot look at somebody else and say, "Why is all this happening to me and everything comes up roses for you?"

Jesus revealed to Peter ahead of time some of the suffering he would go through. Peter immediately wanted to compare his suffering and his lot in life with somebody else's by saying, "What about this man?"

"Jesus said to him, If I want him to stay (survive, live) till I come, what is that to you? [What concern is it of yours?] You follow Me!" (John 21:22).

That is His answer to us also. We are not called to compare, only to comply to His will for us.

❧

God wants you to know that you are unique and that He has an individualized, specialized plan for your life.

GOD'S WORD FOR YOU

Having gifts (faculties, talents, qualities) that differ according to the grace given us, let us use them. . . .

ROMANS 12:6

I have strength for all things in Christ Who empowers me [I am ready for anything and equal to anything through Him Who infuses inner strength into me; I am self-sufficient in Christ's sufficiency].

PHILIPPIANS 4:13

Focus on Potential, Not Limitations

In order to succeed at being yourself, build confidence, and overcome insecurity you must *focus on potential instead of limitations*. In other words, focus on your strengths instead of your weaknesses.

You and I really cannot do *anything* we want to do. We cannot do anything or everything that everyone else is doing. But we can do everything *God has called us to do*. And we can be anything *God says we can be*.

Each of us is full of gifts and talents and potentials and abilities. If we really begin to cooperate with God, we can go for the very best that God has for us. But if we get high-minded ideas and set goals that are beyond our abilities and the grace gifts on our life, we will become frustrated. We will not attain those goals, and we may even end up blaming God for our failure.

Gifts and talents are distributed by the Holy Spirit according to the grace that is on each person to handle them. If you are going to like yourself, if you are going to succeed at being yourself, you are going to have to focus on your potential—what God has created you to be—not on your limitations.

If God has called you to do something,
you will find yourself loving it despite
any adversity that may beset you.

GOD'S WORD FOR YOU

Now am I trying to win the favor of men, or of God? Do I seek to please men? If I were still seeking popularity with men, I should not be a bond servant of Christ (the Messiah).

GALATIANS 1:10

⁂

Not with eyeservice, as menpleasers; but as the servants of Christ, doing the will of God from the heart.

EPHESIANS 6:6 KJV

Have the Courage to Be Different

If you are going to overcome insecurity and be the person you are called to be in Christ, *you must have the courage to be different*. To be a success at being completely and fully you, you are going to have to take a chance on not being like everyone else.

Becoming menpleasers is one of the easiest things we can do but one that can ultimately make us very unhappy. When we begin pleasing other people, we begin to hear comments that make us feel good about ourselves. That is okay as long as we do not derive our sense of worth from it. As believers, our sense of worth has to be rooted and grounded in the love of God.

We are worth something because God sent His only Son to die for us. We are worth something because God loves us, not because of what everybody else thinks about us or says about us.

As followers of Christ, we are to be led by the Spirit, not controlled by people, doing what everybody else wants us to do because we think that will gain us acceptance and approval. In the same manner, we should not try to control others, but allow them to be led by the Spirit just as we are.

Don't put God in a box. He has many ways of leading you if you will permit Him to be the Leader while you become the follower.

GOD'S WORD FOR YOU

But as for you, the anointing (the sacred appointment, the unction) which you received from Him abides [permanently] in you; [so] then you have no need that anyone should instruct you. But just as His anointing teaches you concerning everything and is true and is no falsehood, so you must abide in (live in, never depart from) Him [being rooted in Him, knit to Him], just as [His anointing] has taught you [to do].

1 JOHN 2:27 TLB

LEARN TO COPE WITH CRITICISM

If you are going to overcome insecurity, you have to *learn to cope with criticism.*

Are you a self-validating person, or do you need outside validation? Outside validation is needing somebody to tell you that you are okay. Self-validation is taking action as you are led by the Holy Ghost.

When we hear from God, we often confer too much with people. With the Holy Spirit in us, we do not need to consult with others. The writer of Proverbs says, "In the multitude of counselors there is safety" (Proverbs 11:14). The answer is to be obedient to the Spirit without refusing counsel from others who are wiser than we are.

We must learn to be secure enough to know how to cope with criticism without feeling there is something wrong with us. We must not come under bondage thinking we have to conform to other people's opinions.

Have enough confidence in who you are in Christ that you can listen to others and be open to change without feeling you have to agree with their viewpoint or meet with their approval if you don't feel their suggestion is right for you.

You may have faults, there may be things about you that need to be changed, but God is working on you the same as He is on everybody else.

GOD'S WORD FOR YOU

For we [Christians] are the true circumcision, who worship God in spirit and by the Spirit of God and exult and glory and pride ourselves in Jesus Christ, and put no confidence or dependence [on what we are] in the flesh and on outward privileges and physical advantages and external appearances.

PHILIPPIANS 3:3

Discover the True Source of Confidence

The most important key to becoming more secure is *to discover the true source of confidence.* In what do you place your confidence? That question must be settled before you can ever have God's confidence. Before your confidence can be in Him, you must remove your confidence from other things.

Is God dealing with you about where you have placed your confidence? Is it in marriage? A college degree? Your job? Your spouse? Your children?

We should not place our confidence in our education, our looks, our position, our gifts, our talents, or in other people's opinions. Our heavenly Father is saying to us, "No more; it is time to let go of all those fleshly things you have been holding so firmly for so long. It is time to put your trust and confidence in Me, and Me alone!"

You must come to the place where your confidence is not in the flesh but in Christ Jesus. Learn to trust Him: "Commit your way to the Lord [roll and repose each care of your load on Him]; trust (lean on, rely on, and be confident) also in Him and He will bring it to pass" (Psalm 37:5).

Allow the Lord to shake loose from you the false sense of confidence, worth, security, and well-being you are trying so hard to derive from earthly things.

WHEN YOU FEEL DEPRESSED

To live as God intends for us to live,
the first thing we must do
is truly believe that it is God's will
for us to experience continual joy.

GOD'S WORD FOR YOU

I waited patiently and expectantly for the Lord; and He inclined to me and heard my cry.

He drew me up out of a horrible pit [a pit of tumult and of destruction], out of the miry clay (froth and slime), and set my feet upon a rock, steadying my steps and establishing my goings.

And He has put a new song in my mouth, a song of praise to our God. Many shall see and fear (revere and worship) and put their trust and confident reliance in the Lord. [Ps. 5:11].

PSALM 40:1-3

❦

Be glad in the Lord and rejoice, you [uncompromisingly] righteous [you who are upright and in right standing with Him]; shout for joy, all you upright in heart!

PSALM 32:11

❦

five

WHEN YOU FEEL DEPRESSED

*P*eople from all walks of life have bouts with depression. There are many underlying causes for depression and a variety of treatments offered to deal with it. Some are effective, but many are not. Some help temporarily but can never permanently remove the torment of depression. The good news is that Jesus can heal depression and deliver us from it.

God has given us His joy to fight depression. If you are a believer in Jesus Christ, the joy of the Lord is inside you. Many believers know this but don't have the slightest idea how to tap into that joy or release it. We need to experience what is ours as a result of our faith in Jesus Christ. *It is God's will for us to experience joy!*

I had problems with depression myself a long time ago. But, thank God, I learned I didn't have to allow the negative feeling of depression to rule me. I learned how to release the joy of the Lord in my life!

No matter what you have gone through in life or are going through now, if you are a believer in Jesus Christ, you have His joy inside you, and you can learn how to release it to win over depression.

The reason we can laugh and enjoy life
in spite of our current situation or circumstances
is because Jesus is our joy.

GOD'S WORD FOR YOU

. . . but one thing I do [it is my one aspiration]; forgetting what lies behind and straining forward to what lies ahead.

PHILIPPIANS 3:13

DEAL WITH DISAPPOINTMENT

All of us must face and deal with disappointment at different times. No person alive has everything happen in life the way they want in the way they expect.

When things don't prosper or succeed according to our plan, the first emotion we feel is disappointment. This is normal. There is nothing wrong with feeling disappointed. But we must know what to do with that feeling, or it will move into something more serious.

In the world we cannot live without experiencing disappointment, but in Jesus we can always be given re-appointment!

The apostle Paul stated that one important lesson he had learned in life was to let go of what lay behind and press toward all that lay ahead!

When we get disappointed, then immediately get re-appointed, that's exactly what we're doing. We're letting go of the causes for the disappointment and pressing toward what God has for us. We get a new vision, plan, idea, a fresh outlook, a new mind-set, and we change our focus to that. *We decide to go on!*

Every day is a brand-new start! We can let go of yesterday's disappointments and give God a chance to do something wonderful for us today.

GOD'S WORD FOR YOU

But about midnight, as Paul and Silas were praying and singing hymns of praise to God. . . . Suddenly there was a great earthquake, so that the very foundations of the prison were shaken; and at once all the doors were opened and everyone's shackles were unfastened.

ACTS 16:25-26

Rejoice in the Lord always [delight, gladden yourselves in Him]; again I say, Rejoice!

PHILIPPIANS 4:4

THE POWER OF REJOICING

Throughout the Bible, God instructs His people to be filled with joy and rejoice. The apostle Paul, inspired by the Holy Spirit, instructed the Philippians twice to rejoice. Any time the Lord tells us twice to do something, we need to pay careful attention to what He is saying.

Many times people see or hear the word "rejoice" and say, "That sounds nice, but how do I do that?" They would like to rejoice but don't know how!

Paul and Silas, who had been beaten, thrown into prison, and their feet put in stocks, rejoiced by simply singing praises to God. They chose to rejoice, despite their circumstances.

The same power that opened the doors and broke the shackles off Paul and Silas and those imprisoned with them is available to people today who are imprisoned and shackled with depression.

Joy can be anything from calm delight to extreme hilarity. Joy improves our countenance, our health, and the quality of our lives. It strengthens our witness to others and makes some of the less desirable circumstances in life more bearable.

GOD'S WORD FOR YOU

. . . for the joy of the Lord is your strength and stronghold.

NEHEMIAH 8:10

But none of these things move me; neither do I esteem my life dear to myself, if only I may finish my course with joy and the ministry which I have obtained from [which was entrusted to me by] the Lord Jesus, faithfully to attest to the good news (Gospel) of God's grace (His unmerited favor, spiritual blessing, and mercy).

ACTS 20:24

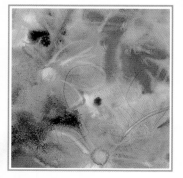

PRIME THE PUMP

When we don't feel joyful, we need to take some action to release joy before we start slipping into depression. Sometimes we must start to rejoice whether we feel like it or not. It is like priming a pump by repeatedly moving the handle up and down until the pump kicks in and the water begins to flow.

I remember my grandparents had an old-time pump. I can recall standing at the sink as a small child moving the pump handle up and down and sometimes feeling as though it would never take hold and start to supply water. It actually felt as if it was connected to nothing, and I was just pumping air.

But if I didn't give up, moving the handle up and down would soon become more difficult. That was a sign that water would start flowing shortly.

This is the way it is with joy. We have a well of water on the inside of our spirit. The pump handle to bring it up is physical exuberance—smiling, singing, laughing, and so forth. At first the physical expressions may not seem to be doing any good. And after a while it even gets harder, but if we keep it up, soon we will get a "gusher" of joy.

If joy is a fruit of the Spirit,
and the Spirit is in you, joy is in you.
What we need to do is learn how to release it.

GOD'S WORD FOR YOU

Why are you cast down, O my inner self? And why should you moan over me and be disquieted within me? Hope in God and wait expectantly for Him, for I shall yet praise Him, my Help and my God.

PSALM 42:5

WAIT EXPECTANTLY FOR GOD

Does your inner man ever feel cast down? Sometimes mine does. So did David's. When he felt that way, David put his hope in God and waited for Him, praising Him as his Help and his God.

To overcome his downcast feelings and emotions, he used songs and shouts of deliverance. That's why so many of his psalms are songs of praise to God to be sung in the midst of unsettling situations.

David knew that when he got down, his countenance went down with him. That is why he talked to himself, his soul (mind, will, and emotions), and encouraged and strengthened himself in the Lord (1 Samuel 30:6).

When we find ourselves in that same depressed state—we should wait expectantly for the Lord, praise Him Who is our Help and our God, and encourage and strengthen ourselves in Him.

We who are righteous—in right standing with God—by believing in Jesus Christ, we who take refuge and put our trust in the Lord can sing and shout for joy! The Lord makes a covering over us and defends us. He fights our battles for us when we praise Him (2 Chronicles 20:17, 20-21)!

You and I must realize and remember that depression is not part of our inheritance in Jesus Christ. It is not part of God's will for His children.

GOD'S WORD FOR YOU

Be well balanced (temperate, sober of mind), be vigilant and cautious at all times; for that enemy of yours, the devil, roams around like a lion roaring [in fierce hunger], seeking someone to seize upon and devour.

Withstand him; be firm in faith [against his onset— rooted, established, strong, immovable, and determined], knowing that the same (identical) sufferings are appointed to your brotherhood (the whole body of Christians) throughout the world.

1 PETER 5:8-9

RESIST DEPRESSION IMMEDIATELY

There are many causes of depression—but only one source: Satan. He wants to keep us pressed down and feeling badly about ourselves so that we won't receive all that Jesus died to give us.

No matter what the causes of depression—physical, mental, emotional, or spiritual—as soon as we feel depression coming on, we need to resist it immediately and take whatever action the Lord leads us to take.

Don't play around with depression. As soon as we start feeling disappointed, we must say to ourselves, "I had better do something about this before it gets worse." If we don't, we will ultimately get discouraged, then depressed. Jesus gave us "the garment of praise for the spirit of heaviness" to put on (Isaiah 61:3 KJV). If we don't use what He has given us, we will sink lower and lower into the pit of depression and could end up in real trouble.

Resisting Satan at his onset will stop extended bouts of depression. We resist the devil by submitting ourselves to God and by wielding the sword of the Spirit, which is His Word (Ephesians 6:17).

Anytime we feel anything that is not part of the will of God for us, that is when we need to begin to wield the sharp, two-edged sword of the Word.

GOD'S WORD FOR YOU

Therefore, [there is] now no condemnation (no adjudging guilty of wrong) for those who are in Christ Jesus, who live [and] walk not after the dictates of the flesh, but after the dictates of the Spirit. [John 3:18.]

ROMANS 8:1

No Condemnation

One of the biggest tools Satan uses to try to make us feel bad is condemnation, which certainly can be a cause of depression. According to this scripture, we who are in Christ Jesus are no longer condemned, no longer judged guilty or wrong. Yet so often we judge and condemn ourselves.

Until I learned and understood the Word of God, I lived a large part of my life feeling guilty. If someone had asked me what I felt guilty about, I could not have answered. All I knew was that there was a vague feeling of guilt that followed me around all the time.

From that experience, God gave me a real revelation about walking free from guilt and condemnation. He showed me that you and I must not only receive forgiveness from Him, we must also forgive ourselves. We must stop beating ourselves over the head for something that He has forgiven and forgotten (Jeremiah 31:34; Acts 10:15).

I believe it is nearly impossible to get depressed if the mind is kept under strict control. That is why we are told in Isaiah 26:3 that God will guard and keep us in perfect and constant peace—if we will keep our mind stayed on Him.

God has new things on the horizon
of your life, but you will never see them
if you live in and relive the past.

GOD'S WORD FOR YOU

*Although my father and my mother have forsaken me,
yet the Lord will take me up [adopt me as His child].*

PSALM 27:10

*See what [an incredible] quality of love the Father has
given (shown, bestowed on) us, that we should [be
permitted to] be named and called and counted the
children of God! And so we are!*

1 JOHN 3:1

GOD DOES NOT REJECT US

Rejection causes depression. To be rejected means to be thrown away as having no value or as being unwanted. We were created for acceptance, not rejection. The emotional pain of rejection is one of the deepest kinds known. Especially if the rejection comes from someone we love or expect to love us, like parents or a spouse.

If you have been depressed, it might be due to a root of rejection in your life. Overcoming rejection is certainly not easy, but we can overcome it through the love of Jesus Christ.

In Ephesians 3:18, Paul prayed for the church that they would know "the breadth and length and height and depth" of the love that God had for them and that they would experience it for themselves. He said this experience far surpasses mere knowledge.

Watch for all the ways that God shows His love for you, and it will overcome the rejection you may have experienced from other people. Every time God gives us favor, He is showing us that He loves us. There are many ways He shows His love for us all the time; we simply need to begin watching for it.

Having a deep revelation concerning God's love for us will keep us from depression.

GOD'S WORD FOR YOU

To the praise of the glory of his grace, wherein he hath made us accepted in the beloved.

EPHESIANS 1:6 KJV

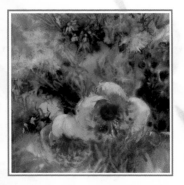

LISTEN TO WHAT GOD SAYS ABOUT YOU

God does not want us to feel frustrated and condemned. He wants us to realize that we are pleasing to Him just as we are.

The devil keeps trying to tell us what we are not, but God keeps trying to tell us what we are—His beloved children who are well-pleasing to Him.

God never reminds us of how far we have fallen. He always reminds us of how far we have risen. He reminds us of how much we have overcome, how precious we are in His sight, how much He loves us.

The devil tells us we cannot possibly be acceptable to God because we are not perfect, but God tells us that we are accepted in the Beloved because of what He has already done for us.

God wants us to know that His hand is upon us, that His angels are watching over us, that His Holy Spirit is right there in us and with us to help us in everything we do.

He wants us to know that Jesus is our Friend, and that as we walk with Him day by day, good things are going to take place in our lives.

If we listen to God rather than the devil,
He will give us peace about the past,
joy for the present, and hope for the future.

WHEN
YOU FEEL
AFRAID

We can live without fear
by building our faith on what
God has said in His Word.

GOD'S WORD FOR YOU

Fear not [there is nothing to fear], for I am with you; do not look around you in terror and be dismayed, for I am your God. I will strengthen and harden you to difficulties, yes, I will help you; yes, I will hold you up and retain you with My [victorious] right hand of rightness and justice.

ISAIAH 41:10

six

WHEN YOU FEEL AFRAID

ne of the benefits available to us in our spiritual inheritance as a believer in Jesus Christ is freedom from fear. But even if we are afraid, we know that we can go ahead and act on what God says, because God will be with us to protect us. He will help us, go before to fight the battle for us or deliver us, bringing us through victoriously as we obey Him.

If you feel you have missed out on some blessings in your life because of fear, you can learn how to handle or overcome fear and begin to experience the abundant life God has planned for you.

The message of "fear not, for I, the Lord, am with you" is expressed in many different ways throughout the Bible. God does not want us to fear because fear prevents us from receiving and doing all He has planned for us. He loves us and wants to bless us, and He has provided ways for us not to fear.

The only acceptable attitude (and confession) that a Christian can have toward fear is this: "It is not from God, and I will not let it control my life! I will confront fear, for it is a spirit sent out from hell to torment me."

God has a plan for your life. Receive His plan by putting your faith in Him. Make a decision today that you will no longer let a spirit of fear intimidate you and dominate your life.

Jesus is your Deliverer. As you diligently seek Him, He will deliver you from all fear.

GOD'S WORD FOR YOU

Fear not; stand still (firm, confident, undismayed) and see the salvation of the Lord which He will work for you today.

EXODUS 14:13

. . . the devil . . . was a murderer from the beginning and does not stand in the truth, because there is no truth in him. When he speaks a falsehood, he speaks what is natural to him, for he is a liar [himself] and the father of lies and of all that is false.

JOHN 8:44

FEAR IS FALSEHOOD

Jesus said that the devil is a liar and the father of all lies. The truth is not in him. He tries to use falsehood to deceive God's people into fear so they will not be bold enough to be obedient to the Lord and reap the blessings He has in store for them.

Often the fear of something is worse than the thing itself. If we will be courageous and determined to do whatever it is we fear, we will discover it is not nearly as bad as we thought it would be.

Throughout the Word of God we find the Lord saying to His people, "Fear not." I believe the reason He did that was to encourage them so they would not allow Satan to rob them of their blessing.

In the same way, because He knows we are fearful, the Lord continues to exhort and encourage us to press through what lies before us to do His will. Why? Because He knows that great blessings await us.

Fear, which is spelled f-e-a-r, stands for *false evidence appearing real*. The enemy wants to tell you that your current situation is evidence that your future will be a failure, but the Bible teaches us that no matter what our present circumstances, nothing is impossible with God (Mark 9:17-23).

Only when you know God's Word will you recognize the lies of Satan. Confess the Word of God, and it will bring you into a place of victory.

GOD'S WORD FOR YOU

For God did not give us a spirit of timidity (of cowardice, of craven and cringing and fawning fear), but [He has given us a spirit] of power and of love and of calm and well-balanced mind and discipline and self-control.

2 TIMOTHY 1:7

No Fear!

Every one of us has experienced starting to step out in faith, and even at the thought of it, fear begins to rise up in us. We need to realize that the source of fear is Satan. First John 4:18 KJV says: "There is no fear in love; but perfect love casteth out fear: because fear hath torment. He that feareth is not made perfect in love."

Satan sends fear to try to torment us into being so doubtful and miserable so that we will be prevented from doing what God wants us to do and receiving all that God has for us.

We can live without fear by building our faith on what God has said in His Word. When we open our mouth and confess what the Lord says to us and about us, God's Word will give us the power to overcome the fears that torment and prevent.

When we find ourselves trying to avoid confronting some issue in our life because of fear or dread or wondering or reasoning, we should pray and ask God to do for us what He has promised in His Word—to go before us and pave the way for us.

Ask God to strengthen you in the inner man, that His might and power may fill you, and that you may not be overcome with the temptation to give in to fear.

G O D ' S   W O R D   F O R   Y O U

For [the Spirit which] you have now received [is] not a spirit of slavery to put you once more in bondage to fear, but you have received the Spirit of adoption [the Spirit producing sonship] in [the bliss of] which we cry, Abba (Father)! Father!

ROMANS 8:15

I WILL NOT FEAR!

Fear robs many people of their faith.

Fear of failure, fear of man, and fear of rejection are some of the strongest fears employed by Satan to hinder us from making progress. But no matter what kind of fear the enemy sends against us, the important thing is to overcome it. When we are faced with fear, we must not give in to it. It is imperative to our victory that we determine, "I will not fear!"

The normal reaction to fear is flight. Satan wants us to run; God wants us to stand still and see His deliverance.

Because of fear, many people do not confront issues; they spend their lives running. We must learn to stand our ground and face fear, secure in the knowledge that we are more than conquerors (Romans 8:37).

Fear of failure torments multitudes. We fear what people will think of us if we fail. If we step out and fail, some people may hear about it; but they quickly forget if we forget it and go on. It is better to try something and fail than to try nothing and succeed.

Approach life with boldness. The Spirit of the Lord is in you — so make up your mind not to fear.

GOD'S WORD FOR YOU

The earnest (heartfelt, continued) prayer of a righteous man makes tremendous power available [dynamic in its working].

JAMES 5:16

PRAY ABOUT EVERYTHING AND FEAR NOTHING

Some time ago the Lord spoke these words to me: "Pray about everything and fear nothing." Over the next couple of weeks, He showed me different things about prayer versus fear. Many of them dealt with little areas in which fear would try to creep into my life and cause me problems. He showed me that in every case, no matter how great or important or how small or insignificant, the solution was to pray.

Sometimes we become afraid by staring at our circumstances. The more we focus on the problem, the more fearful we become. Instead, we are to keep our focus on God. He is able to handle anything that we may ever have to face in this life.

God has promised to strengthen us, to harden us to difficulties, to hold us up and retain us with His victorious right hand. He also commands us not to be afraid. But remember, He is not commanding us never to feel fear, but rather not to let it control us.

The Lord is saying to you and me personally, "Fear not, I will help you." But we never experience the help of God until we place everything on the line, until we are obedient enough to step out in faith.

❧

When you feel fear, don't back down or run away. Instead, pray and go forward even though you are afraid.

GOD'S WORD FOR YOU

If any of you is deficient in wisdom, let him ask of the giving God [Who gives] to everyone liberally and ungrudgingly, without reproaching or faultfinding, and it will be given him.

Only it must be in faith that he asks with no wavering (no hesitating, no doubting). For the one who wavers (hesitates, doubts) is like the billowing surge out at sea that is blown hither and thither and tossed by the wind.

For truly, let not such a person imagine that he will receive anything [he asks for] from the Lord.

JAMES 1:5-7

FAITH: THE ANTIDOTE FOR FEAR

Faith is the only antidote for fear.

If you or I drank some kind of poison, we would have to swallow an antidote, or the poison would cause serious damage or even death. The same is true of the deadly toxin of fear. There must be an antidote for it, and the only antidote for fear is faith.

When fear comes knocking at our door, we must answer it with faith, because nothing else is effective against it. And prayer is the major vehicle that carries faith.

Faith must be carried to the problem and released in some way. It is possible to pray without faith (we do it all the time), but it is impossible to have real faith and *not* pray.

James tells us that when we find ourselves in need of something, we should pray and ask God for it in *simple, believing* prayer. Those two words are very important. The way we do that is by simply praying and having faith, believing that what we ask for from God we will receive in accordance with His divine will and plan.

Put your faith in the Lord.
He has the power to deliver you from all fear.

GOD'S WORD FOR YOU

Now [in Haran] the Lord said to Abram, Go for yourself [for your own advantage] away from your country, from your relatives and your father's house, to the land that I will show you.

GENESIS 12:1

Do It Afraid!

How would you feel if God told you to leave your home, your family, and everything familiar and comfortable to you and head out to who knows where? Full of fear? That is precisely the challenge Abram faced, and it frightened him. That's why God kept saying to him again and again, "Fear not."

Elisabeth Elliot, whose husband was killed along with four other missionaries in Ecuador, tells that her life was controlled completely by fear. Every time she started to step out, fear stopped her. A friend told her something that set her free. She said, "Why don't you do it afraid?" Elisabeth Elliot and Rachel Saint, sister of one of the murdered missionaries, went on to evangelize the Indian tribes, including the people who had killed their husband and brother.

If we wait to do something until we are not afraid, we will probably accomplish very little for God, others, or even for ourselves. Both Abram and Joshua had to step out in faith and obedience to God and do what He had commanded them to do—afraid. We must do the same!

Be determined that your life is not going to be ruled by fear but by God's Word.

GOD'S WORD FOR YOU

After these things, the word of the Lord came to Abram in a vision, saying, Fear not, Abram, I am your Shield, your abundant compensation, and your reward shall be exceedingly great.

GENESIS 15:1

COURAGE AND OBEDIENCE PRODUCE GREAT REWARDS

In Genesis 12:1, God gave Abram a tall order. In so many words He said, "Pack up and leave everyone you know and everything you are comfortable with and go to a place I will show you."

If Abram had bowed his knee to fear, the rest of the story would never have come to pass. He would never have experienced God as his Shield, his great compensation, and he would never have received his exceedingly great reward.

In the same way, if Joshua had not overcome his fear and been obedient to God's command to lead His people into the Promised Land, neither he nor they would ever have enjoyed all that God had planned and prepared for them.

There is power in God's Word to equip us to stop bowing our knee in fear to the devil's desires. We can do what God wants us to do, even if we have to do it afraid. We need to keep saying: "Lord, strengthen me. This is what You have told me to do, and with Your help I am going to do it, because it is Your revealed will for me. I am determined that my life is not going to be ruled by fear but by Your Word."

God doesn't always deliver us "from" things;
often He walks us "through" them.

GOD'S WORD FOR YOU

So we take comfort and are encouraged and confidently and boldly say, The Lord is my Helper; I will not be seized with alarm [I will not fear or dread or be terrified]. What can man do to me?

HEBREWS 13:6

COMBAT FEAR WITH PRAYER

Fear attacks everyone. It is Satan's way of tormenting us and preventing us from enjoying the life Jesus died to give us. If we accept the fears that Satan offers and give voice to them, we open the door for the enemy and close the door to God.

We must learn as David and the writer of Hebrews to boldly confess that God is our Helper, our Refuge, and our Stronghold.

Satan seeks to weaken us through fear, but God strengthens us as we fellowship with Him in prayer. The Bible teaches us to watch and pray: "All of you must keep awake (give strict attention, be cautious and active) and watch and pray, that you may not come into temptation. The spirit indeed is willing, but the flesh is weak" (Matthew 26:41). The major reference in this passage is to watching ourselves and the attacks that the enemy launches against our minds and our emotions. When these attacks are detected, we should pray immediately. We must remember that it is when we pray that power is released against the enemy—not when we think about praying later.

Watch and pray about everything. I believe you will find this decision to be one that will produce more joy and peace for your everyday living.

If we are ever to have real victory over the enemy, we must resist him in prayer with faith.

THE POWER OF
BEING POSITIVE

THE POWER
OF BEING
POSITIVE

Positive minds produce positive lives.
Positive thoughts are always
full of faith and hope.

GOD'S WORD FOR YOU

For as he thinks in his heart, so is he.

PROVERBS 23:7

Then to the centurion Jesus said, Go; it shall be done for you as you have believed. And the servant boy was restored to health at that very moment.

MATTHEW 8:13

one

THE POWER OF BEING POSITIVE

any years ago, I was an extremely negative person. My whole philosophy was this: "If you don't expect anything good to happen, then you won't be disappointed when it doesn't." So many devastating things had happened to me over the years that I was afraid to believe that anything good might happen. Since my thoughts were all negative, so was my mouth; therefore, so was my life.

Perhaps you're like me. You're avoiding hope to protect yourself against being hurt. This type of behavior sets up a negative lifestyle. Everything becomes negative because the thoughts are negative.

When I really began to study the Word and to trust God to restore me, one of the first things I realized was that the negativism had to go. And the longer I serve God, the more I realize the tremendous power in being positive in my thoughts and words.

Our actions are a direct result of our thoughts. A negative mind will result in a negative life. But if we renew our mind according to God's Word, we will, as Romans 12:2 promises, prove in our experience "the good and acceptable and perfect will of God."

It is a vital necessity that we line up our thoughts with God's thoughts. This is a process that will take time and study.

135

GOD'S WORD FOR YOU

We are assured and know that [God being a partner in their labor] all things work together and are [fitting into a plan] for good to and for those who love God and are called according to [His] design and purpose.

ROMANS 8:28

ALL THINGS WORK FOR GOOD

The apostle Paul does not say that all things are good, but he does say that all things *work together for good*.

Let's say you get in your car, and it won't start. There are two ways you can look at the situation. You can say, "I knew it! It never fails. My plans always flop." Or you can say, "Well, it looks as though I can't leave right now. I'll go later when the car is fixed. In the meantime, I believe this change in plans is going to work out for my good. There is probably some reason I need to be at home today, so I'm going to enjoy my time here."

Paul also tells us in Romans 12:16 to "readily adjust yourself to [people, things]." The idea is that we must learn to become the kind of person who plans things but who doesn't fall apart if that plan doesn't work out.

The choice is ours. Any time we don't get what we want, our feelings will rise up and try to get us into self-pity and a negative attitude. Or we can adjust to the situation and go ahead and enjoy what God has for us no matter what happens.

❧

The pathway to freedom from negativity begins when we face the problem without making excuses for it.

GOD'S WORD FOR YOU

Therefore if any person is [ingrafted] in Christ (the Messiah) he is a new creation (a new creature altogether); the old [previous moral and spiritual condition] has passed away. Behold, the fresh and new has come!

2 CORINTHIANS 5:17

A New Day

As "a new creation," you don't have to allow the old things that happened to you to keep affecting your new life in Christ. You are a new creature with a new life in Christ. You can have your mind renewed according to the Word of God. Good things are going to happen to you!

Begin to think positively about your life. That doesn't mean that you can get anything you want by just thinking about it. God has a perfect plan for each of us, and we can't control Him with our thoughts and words. But, we must think and speak in agreement with His will and plan for us.

If you don't have any idea what God's will is for you at this point, at least begin by thinking, *Well, I don't know God's plan, but I know He loves me. Whatever He does will be good, and I'll be blessed.*

The hardest part is saying to yourself, "I want to change. I can't change myself, but I believe God will change me as I trust Him. I know it will take time, and I'm not going to get discouraged with myself. *God has begun a good work in me, and He is well able to bring it to full completion*" (see Philippians 1:6).

Jesus will set you free to enjoy the good things in life. Trust God to renew your mind with His Word!

GOD'S WORD FOR YOU

However, I am telling you nothing but the truth when I say it is profitable (good, expedient, advantageous) for you that I go away. Because if I do not go away, the Comforter (Counselor, Helper, Advocate, Intercessor, Strengthener, Standby) will not come to you [into close fellowship with you]; but if I go away, I will send Him to you [to be in close fellowship with you].

And when He comes, He will convict and convince the world and bring demonstration to it about sin and about righteousness (uprightness of heart and right standing with God) and about judgment.

JOHN 16:7–8

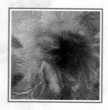

TRUST THE HOLY SPIRIT

Even though I was extremely negative, and although I struggled to keep my mind in a positive pattern, God showed me that if I would trust Him, He would cause me to be very positive. Now, I can't stand negativism. It's similar to the experience of a person who quits smoking and then has no tolerance for cigarettes. I've seen so many good changes in my life since I've been delivered from a negative mind that now I'm opposed to anything negative.

Here's what you need to do. Ask the Holy Spirit to convict you each time you start to get negative. This is part of His work. John 16:7–8 teaches us that the Holy Spirit will convict us of sin and convince us of righteousness. When the conviction comes, ask God to help you. Don't think you can handle this yourself. Lean on Him.

Face reality. If you are sick, don't say, "I'm not sick," because that's just not true. But you can say, "I believe God is healing me." You don't have to say, "I'll probably get worse and end up in the hospital." You can say, "God's healing power is working right now. I believe I'll be all right."

Bring your life into a healthy balance. Ask God to help you have a "ready mind" to deal with whatever happens to you, whether it is positive or negative.

141

GOD'S WORD FOR YOU

These were more noble than those in Thessalonica, in that they received the word with all readiness of mind, and searched the scriptures daily, whether those things were so.

ACTS 17:11 KJV

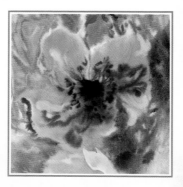

 READY MIND

The Bible says that we are to have a ready mind. That means we are to have minds that are open to the will of God for us, whatever that will may be.

Recently a young lady whom I know experienced the sorrow of a broken engagement. She wanted the relationship to continue and was thinking, hoping, and believing that her former fiancé would feel the same way.

I advised her to have a "ready mind" in case it didn't work out that way. She asked, "Well, isn't that being negative?"

No, it isn't! Negativism would say, "My life is over. No one will ever want me. I'll be miserable forever."

Having a positive mind says, "I'm really sad this happened, but I'm going to trust God. I'm going to ask and believe for our relationship to be restored; but more than anything, I want God's perfect will. If it doesn't turn out the way I want, I'll survive, because Jesus lives in me. It may be hard, but I trust the Lord. I believe that in the end everything will work out for the best."

Practice being positive in every situation that arises.
God has promised to bring good out of whatever
is taking place in your life at the moment.

GOD'S WORD FOR YOU

[For Abraham, human reason for] hope being gone, hoped in faith that he should become the father of many nations, as he had been promised, So [numberless] shall your descendants be.

He did not weaken in faith when he considered the [utter] impotence of his own body, which was as good as dead because he was about a hundred years old, or [when he considered] the barrenness of Sarah's [deadened] womb.

No unbelief or distrust made him waver (doubtingly question) concerning the promise of God, but he grew strong and was empowered by faith as he gave praise and glory to God.

ROMANS 4:18–20

THE FORCE OF HOPE

In our ministry we want to help more people every year, and we believe God wants us to grow. But we also realize that if God has a different plan, and if we end our year with no growth, we cannot let that situation control our joy.

We believe *for* many things, but beyond them all, we believe *in* Someone. That Someone is Jesus. We don't always know what is going to happen. We just know it will always work out for our good!

It is reported that Abraham, after sizing up his situation (he didn't ignore the facts), considered the utter impotence of his own body and the barrenness of Sarah's womb. Although all human reason for hope was gone, he hoped in faith.

Abraham was very positive about a very negative situation!

Hebrews 6:19 tells us that hope is the anchor of the soul. Hope is the force that keeps us steady in a time of trial. Don't ever stop hoping. If you do, you're going to have a miserable life. Don't be afraid to hope. No one can promise that you'll never be disappointed. But you can always have hope and be positive. Put yourself in God's miracle-working realm.

Expect a miracle in your life!

GOD'S WORD FOR YOU

And therefore the Lord [earnestly] waits [expecting, looking, and longing] to be gracious to you; and therefore He lifts Himself up, that He may have mercy on you and show loving-kindness to you. For the Lord is a God of justice. Blessed (happy, fortunate, to be envied) are all those who [earnestly] wait for Him, who expect and look and long for Him [for His victory, His favor, His love, His peace, His joy, and His matchless, unbroken companionship]!

ISAIAH 30:18

EXPECT TO RECEIVE!

I want to establish firmly in your heart forever that you need to begin to think about what you are thinking about. So many people's problems are rooted in thinking patterns that actually produce the problems they experience in their lives. Remember that your actions are the direct result of your thoughts. And although Satan offers wrong thinking to everyone, you don't need to accept his offer.

Isaiah 30:18 has become one of my favorite Scriptures. If you will meditate on it, it will begin to bring you great hope . . . and great power. In it, God is saying that He is looking for someone to be gracious (good) to, but it cannot be someone with a sour attitude and a negative mind. It must be someone who is expecting (looking and longing) for God to be good to him or her.

Don't ever give up, because little by little you are changing. The more you change your mind for the better, the more your life will also change for the better. When you begin to see God's plan for you in your thinking, you will begin to walk in it.

The mind is the leader or forerunner of all actions. Always expect good things from God!

GOD'S WORD FOR YOU

All the days of the desponding and afflicted are made evil [by anxious thoughts and forebodings], but he who has a glad heart has a continual feast [regardless of circumstances].

PROVERBS 15:15

EVIL FOREBODINGS

An "evil foreboding" is a vague, threatening feeling that something bad is going to happen. There was a point when I realized that I had actually carried these feelings with me most of my life. In fact, I had been made miserable by evil thoughts and forebodings.

Perhaps you have these feelings as well. You have circumstances that are very difficult, but even when you don't, you are still miserable because your thoughts are poisoning your outlook and robbing you of the ability to enjoy life and see good days.

Proverbs 15:15 promises us that these feelings need not remain. Faith's attitude is one of leaning on God, trusting and being confident in Him—it is a joyful feasting on the expectancy of good. Rather than dreading something by anticipating that it will make us miserable, we can have faith that God will give us the power to enjoy it.

Our joy, peace, righteousness, and power are on the *inside* of us through the presence of the Holy Spirit. We need to allow Him to work in power on the *inside* and put less focus on the things *outside* us.

*God's power can fall on us and energize us
to do mundane, everyday tasks with great joy.*

GOD'S WORD FOR YOU

For let him who wants to enjoy life and see good days [good—whether apparent or not] keep his tongue free from evil and his lips from guile (treachery, deceit).

1 Peter 3:10

Death and life are in the power of the tongue, and they who indulge in it shall eat the fruit of it [for death or life].

Proverbs 18:21

Keep Your Tongue from Evil

The apostle Peter plainly tells us that enjoying life and seeing good days, and having a positive mind and mouth, are linked together.

Our mouth gives expression to what we think, feel, and want. Our minds tells us what we think, not necessarily what God thinks. Our will tells us what we want, not what God wants. Our emotions tell us what we feel, not what God feels. As our soul is purified, it is trained to carry God's thoughts, desires, and feelings; then we become a mouthpiece for the Lord!

Your words, as reflections of your thoughts, have the power to bring blessing or destruction not only to your life but also to the lives of many others. In 1 Corinthians 2:16, the Word of God teaches us that we have the mind of Christ and that we hold the thoughts, feelings, and purposes of His heart. We hold them in us, but the flesh often blocks them from coming forth. Therein lies the battle—the continual struggle between our flesh and the spirit.

No matter how negative you are or how long you have been that way, I know you can change because I did. It took time and "heaping helpings" of the Holy Spirit, but it was worth it.

The
Battle for
the Mind

The mind is the battlefield
where our war with Satan
is either won or lost.

GOD'S WORD FOR YOU

For we are not wrestling with flesh and blood [contending only with physical opponents], but against the despotisms, against the powers, against [the master spirits who are] the world rulers of this present darkness, against the spirit forces of wickedness in the heavenly (supernatural) sphere.

EPHESIANS 6:12

two

THE BATTLE FOR THE MIND

 careful study of Ephesians 6 informs us that we are in a war, and that our warfare is not with other human beings but with the devil and his demons. Our enemy, Satan, attempts to defeat us with strategy and deceit, through well-laid plans and deliberate deception.

Jesus called the devil "the father of lies and of all that is false" (John 8:44). He lies to you and me. He tells us things about ourselves, about other people, and about circumstances that are just not true. He does not, however, tell us the entire lie all at one time.

He begins by bombarding our mind with a cleverly devised pattern of little nagging thoughts, suspicions, doubts, fears, wonderings, reasonings, and theories. He moves slowly and cautiously. Remember, he has a strategy for his warfare. He has studied us for a long time.

Satan knows what we like and what we don't like. He knows our insecurities, weaknesses, and fears. He knows what bothers us most and is willing to invest any amount of time it takes to defeat us. His strong point is patience.

God intends to work through us to defeat the enemy.
He will do it through us!

GOD'S WORD FOR YOU

*For the weapons of our warfare are not physical
[weapons of flesh and blood], but they are mighty before
God for the overthrow and destruction of strongholds,*

*[Inasmuch as we] refute arguments and theories and
reasonings and every proud and lofty thing that sets itself
up against the [true] knowledge of God; and we lead every
thought and purpose away captive into the obedience of
Christ (the Messiah, the Anointed One) . . .*

2 CORINTHIANS 10:4–5

TEARING DOWN STRONGHOLDS

Through careful strategy and cunning deceit, Satan attempts to set up "strongholds" in our mind. A stronghold is an area in which we are held in bondage (in prison) due to a certain way of thinking. Strongholds are lies that are believed.

The apostle Paul tells us that we have the spiritual weapons we need to overcome Satan's strongholds. Using our weapons, we refute the enemy's lies, arguments, theories, reasonings, and every other thing that tries to exalt itself against the truth of God's Word. We must take our thoughts captive and refuse to indulge in the fleshly luxury of receiving and meditating on every thought that falls into our heads.

The primary weapon with which we do battle is the Word of God used in various ways—preached, taught, sung, confessed, meditated upon, written, and read. We must get the knowledge of God's truth in us to renew our minds. The Word of God has a cleansing effect on our minds and lives any way we use it.

No one will ever live a truly victorious life without being a sincere student of God's Word.

Every stronghold in your mind can be torn down and every deception uncovered. You can win the battle. Don't settle for anything less than complete freedom.

GOD'S WORD FOR YOU

And take the helmet of salvation and the sword that the Spirit wields, which is the Word of God.

EPHESIANS 6:17

If you abide in My word [hold fast to My teachings and live in accordance with them], you are truly My disciples.

And you will know the Truth, and the Truth will set you free.

JOHN 8:31–32

THE SWORD OF THE SPIRIT

The attacks of Satan against the church are more intense than ever before. More people than ever are experiencing tremendous attacks against their minds and enduring great attacks of fear.

A person who learns to abide in the Word of God and let the Word abide in him will have a two-edged sword with which to do battle. To abide means to remain, to continue in, or to dwell in. If you make God's Word a small part of your life, you will know only a partial truth and will experience only limited freedom, but those who *abide* in it will know the full truth and will experience complete freedom.

I can testify that the Word of God has caused me to be victorious over the devil. My life was a mess because I was ignorant of the Word. I had been a Christian for many years who loved God and was active in church work. But I had zero victory because I did not know the Word.

Learn the Word and allow the Holy Spirit to wield it by speaking, singing, or meditating on the portions of Scripture that you feel He is placing on your heart.

If you keep your sword drawn, the enemy won't be so quick to approach you. Speak the Word!

GOD'S WORD FOR YOU

Pray at all times (on every occasion, in every season) in the Spirit, with all [manner of] prayer and entreaty. To that end keep alert and watch with strong purpose and perseverance, interceding in behalf of all the saints (God's consecrated people).

EPHESIANS 6:18

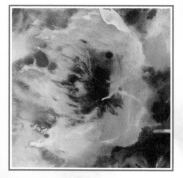

PRAYING IN THE SPIRIT

Prayer is another spiritual weapon God has given us to wage warfare. Prayer is relationship with the Godhead. It is coming and asking for help or talking to God about something that bothers us.

If you want to have an effective prayer life, develop a good personal relationship with the Father. Know that He loves you, that He is full of mercy, that He will help you. Get to know Jesus. He is your Friend. He died for you. Get to know the Holy Spirit. He is with you all the time as your Helper. Let Him help you.

All kinds of prayer are to be used in our walk with God. There is the prayer of agreement between two people and also the united prayer of a group of people. There are prayers of thanksgiving, praise and worship, petition, intercession, commitment, and consecration.

Whatever kind of prayer you bring, learn to fill your prayers with the Word of God and offer them with the assurance that God keeps His Word. God's Word and our need are the basis on which we come to Him.

The more time a person spends meditating on the Word, the more he will reap from the Word.

GOD'S WORD FOR YOU

Let the saints be joyful in the glory and beauty [which God confers upon them]; let them sing for joy upon their beds.

Let the high praises of God be in their throats and a two-edged sword in their hands.

PSALM 149:5–6

HIGH PRAISES OF GOD

In David's Psalm 149, he gives us a picture of the position that the saints of God should take—with songs of praise and worship in their throats and the two-edged sword of the Word of God in their hands. In the remainder of the psalm, he goes on to infer that this position is taken by the saints in order to defeat their enemies.

Praise defeats the devil quicker than any other battle plan. Praise is a garment that we put on and that will protect us from defeat and negativity in our minds. But it must be genuine heart praise, not just lip service or a method being tried to see if it works. Also, praise involves the Word. We praise God according to His Word and His goodness.

Worship is a battle position! As we worship God for Who He is and for His attributes, for His ability and might, we will see His power and attributes released on our behalf.

I am sure your heart frequently fills up with love and worship for God. Bow your heart and give thanks to Him. Praise and worship confuse the enemy. Take your position, and you will see the enemy's defeat.

***

God never loses a battle. He has a definite battle plan, and when we follow it, we always win.

GOD'S WORD FOR YOU

For no temptation (no trial regarded as enticing to sin, no matter how it comes or where it leads) has overtaken you and laid hold on you that is not common to man [that is, no temptation or trial has come to you that is beyond human resistance and that is not adjusted and adapted and belonging to human experience, and such as man can bear]. But God is faithful [to His Word and to His compassionate nature], and He [can be trusted] not to let you be tempted and tried and assayed beyond your ability and strength of resistance and power to endure, but with the temptation He will [always] also provide the way out (the means of escape to a landing place), that you may be capable and strong and powerful to bear up under it patiently.

1 CORINTHIANS 10:13

Never an Excuse

Sadly, many people do not always accept the truth that God reveals to them. It is painful to face our faults and deal with them. We tend to justify misbehavior. We allow our past and how we were raised to negatively affect the rest of our lives.

Our past may explain why we're suffering, but we must not use it as an excuse to stay in bondage.

Everyone is without excuse because Jesus always stands ready to fulfill His promise to set us free. He will walk us across the finish line in any area if we are willing to go all the way through it with Him.

Thank God, we have the weapons to tear down the strongholds. God doesn't abandon us and leave us helpless. He promises us that He will not allow us to be tempted beyond what we can bear, but with every temptation He will also provide the way out, the escape.

You may have some major strongholds in your life that need to be broken. Let me encourage you by saying, "God is on your side." In the spiritual battle going on in your mind, God is fighting on your side.

No matter how great the temptation before us, God has promised us everything we need to walk in victory.

GOD'S WORD FOR YOU

Behold! I have given you authority and power to trample upon serpents and scorpions, and [physical and mental strength and ability] over all the power that the enemy [possesses]; and nothing shall in any way harm you.

LUKE 10:19

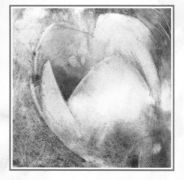

You Have the Power

Far too many believers are fainthearted, weak in determination, and diseased with an "I can't" attitude. They are plagued with a lack of spiritual power.

You and I don't have to beg God to give us power. We just need to realize and accept that we have been given power and then walk in what is already ours. We must develop and maintain a "power consciousness"— an aggressive, power-packed attitude.

God has given us spiritual power for spiritual warfare. Spiritual power is released when our faith is firm. When we walk in faith we can approach every situation with an enemy-conquering attitude.

An attitude of confidence will exude from us when we know who we are in Christ, and believe in the power that the Bible says is ours through faith.

Do you desire to be a powerful believer? Try approaching every situation in your life with a simple, childlike faith—believing that God is good, that He has a good plan for your life, and that He is working in your situation.

***

You have the power and authority of the name of Jesus.
Walk in the strength of His conquering name!

GOD'S WORD FOR YOU

For those who are according to the flesh and are controlled by its unholy desires set their minds on and pursue those things which gratify the flesh, but those who are according to the Spirit and are controlled by the desires of the Spirit set their minds on and seek those things which gratify the [Holy] Spirit.

ROMANS 8:5

Who Controls the Mind?

In the *King James Version*, the eighth chapter of Romans teaches us that if we "mind" the flesh, we will walk in the flesh. But if we "mind" the things of the Spirit, we will walk in the Spirit.

Let me put it another way: If we think fleshly thoughts, wrong thoughts, negative thoughts, we cannot walk in the Spirit. It seems as if renewed, godlike thinking is a vital necessity to a successful Christian life.

Your life may be in a state of chaos because of years of wrong thinking. If so, it is important for you to come to grips with the fact that *your life will not get straightened out until your mind does*. You should consider this area one of *vital necessity*.

You cannot overcome your situation by determination alone. You do need to be determined, but determined in the Holy Spirit, not in the effort of your own flesh. The Holy Spirit is your Helper—seek His help. Lean on Him. You can't make it alone.

❧

Give the Holy Spirit control of your life. He will lead you into the perfect will of God for you, which includes exceeding, abundant blessings, peace, and joy.

GOD'S WORD FOR YOU

Either make the tree sound (healthy and good), and its fruit sound (healthy and good), or make the tree rotten (diseased and bad), and its fruit rotten (diseased and bad); for the tree is known and recognized and judged by its fruit.

MATTHEW 12:33

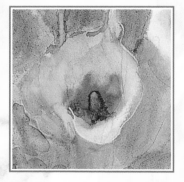

A VITAL NECESSITY

For the believer, right thinking is something that is so important that one simply cannot live without it—like a heartbeat is vital, or blood pressure is vital. There are things without which there is no life. Our life source, our source for right thinking, is regular, personal fellowship with God in prayer and the Word.

The Bible says that a tree is known by its fruit.

The same is true of our lives. Thoughts bear fruit. Think good thoughts, and the fruit of your life will be good. Think bad thoughts, and the fruit in your life will be bad.

Actually, you can look at a person's attitude and know what kind of thinking is prevalent in his life. A sweet, kind person does not have mean, vindictive thoughts. By the same token, a truly evil person does not have good, loving thoughts.

Remember Proverbs 23:7 and allow it to have an impact on your life: for as you think in your heart, so are you.

When we wait in God's presence, there is a divine exchange. We exchange our nothingness for His everything. Our weakness is swallowed up in His strength.

A Heart That Hinders

*While the world is busy trying
to conquer "outer space," we should
strive to conquer "inner space."*

GOD'S WORD FOR YOU

Keep thy heart with all diligence; for out of it are the issues of life.

PROVERBS 4:23 KJV

Amaziah was twenty-five years old when he began to reign, and he reigned twenty-nine years in Jerusalem. . . .
He did right in the Lord's sight, but not with a perfect or blameless heart.

2 CHRONICLES 25:1–2

three

A HEART THAT HINDERS

 hen God speaks to us about our heart, He is asking for our entire life, the entire personality, character, body, mind, and emotions in the spirit of a person. The heart is the real person, not the person everybody sees.

The heart is the most important aspect of the spiritual body, and the heart attitude should be the major issue of every believer. It is not lack of ability or potential that prevents most people from making progress and enjoying fulfillment in life. It is wrong heart attitudes that negatively affect our minds and thoughts.

There are many conditions of the heart. Some are positive, and some are negative. King Amaziah is noted for having a negative condition of the heart. He did all the right things, but his heart was not right. Therefore, God was not pleased with him. That's a scary thing. We can do the right thing, and yet have it not be acceptable to God because we do it with a wrong heart attitude.

God is more concerned about your heart than He is about what you do, because if your heart is right, what you do will eventually catch up with that. Who you are in your heart is reflected in your thoughts and attitudes.

GOD'S WORD FOR YOU

The Lord saw that the wickedness of man was great in the earth, and that every imagination and intention of all human thinking was only evil continually.

And the Lord regretted that He had made man on the earth, and He was grieved at heart.

So the Lord said, I will destroy, blot out, and wipe away mankind, whom I have created from the face of the ground. . . .

But Noah found grace (favor) in the eyes of the Lord.

GENESIS 6:5–8

An Evil Heart

The story of Noah tells us that many people today are being destroyed for the simple reason that their hearts are wrong. There were three heart issues concerning the people of Noah's day that displeased God: wickedness, evil imaginations, and evil thinking. But Noah had a right heart and found favor in the eyes of the Lord.

We cannot imagine how many areas of our lives would get straightened out if we would just get our hearts right with God. Our hearts may not be filled with the exact same evil thoughts and imaginations of the people in Noah's day, but a bad attitude or wrong thinking can also be labeled evil imaginations and evil thinking. If we have a bad attitude and "stinking thinking," we are going nowhere in life.

This is why we must guard our heart—because out of it flow the issues of our life. Our problem is that if we let garbage in, garbage will come back out. Allowing negative, evil thinking in our hearts cannot produce a life that glorifies God. We have to be careful not only about our actions but also about our imagination, our intent, our motivation, our attitude. If we fail here, we may end up with an evil heart.

We need a tender heart that deals immediately with a bad attitude about anything or anyone.

GOD'S WORD FOR YOU

Therefore, as the Holy Spirit says: Today, if you will hear His voice,

Do not harden your hearts, as [happened] in the rebellion [of Israel] and their provocation and embitterment [of Me] in the day of testing in the wilderness.

HEBREWS 3:7–8

[Therefore beware] brethren, take care, lest there be in any one of you a wicked, unbelieving heart [which refuses to cleave to, trust in, and rely on Him], leading you to turn away and desert or stand aloof from the living God.

HEBREWS 3:12

A HARD, UNBELIEVING HEART

In Hebrews 3 we see two wrong conditions of the heart—a hard heart and an unbelieving heart. In the wilderness, a hard heart caused the Israelites to rebel. A person with a hard heart cannot believe God easily, which is a major problem because everything we receive from God comes through believing. To receive from Him, we must come to Him in simple, childlike faith and just believe.

We call ourselves believers, but the truth is, there are a lot of "unbelieving believers." For a long time, I was one of them. I had been hurt so much during my childhood, I developed a hardness of heart that God had to break through in my life.

Even Moses got to the place in the wilderness where he was slow of heart to believe God. That's why we have to stay sharp spiritually if we are going to be quick to believe and to walk in faith day by day. We must be careful to go from faith to faith and not begin to mix in any doubt and unbelief.

Remember that Jesus wants to restore your soul, including your emotions. Let Jesus into those areas of your life that no one else could ever reach. Ask Him to change you into a person after His heart, a person who has the same kind of heart that He has.

GOD'S WORD FOR YOU

. . . he who has a haughty look and a proud and arrogant heart I cannot and I will not tolerate.

PSALM 101:5

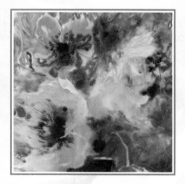

 A Proud Heart

Has God ever had to deal with you about pride? From personal experience I can tell you that a proud person hates to admit his problem with pride.

How can you tell if you have a problem with pride? If you have an opinion about everything, if you are judgmental, if you can't be corrected, if you rebel against authority, if you want to take all the credit for yourself, or if you say "I" too often, you have a problem with pride.

It is hard to let God get all that pride stuff out of us, but it is vital. If we want to experience the power of being positive, we must realize it flows out of an attitude of humility. When we recognize we are not always right about everything, it makes us teachable and willing to take correction. It is only in the place of humility that God can bless us.

The enemy will attack and tempt you with a spirit of pride. It takes effort to keep a right heart. One of the most powerful things we have to guard against is a spirit of self-righteousness.

We have it backward if we think that everything in our life would be fine if the devil just left us alone. If we live right, the devil has no power over us.

GOD'S WORD FOR YOU

Therefore you have no excuse or defense or justification, O man, whoever you are who judges and condemns another. For in posing as judge and passing sentence on another, you condemn yourself, because you who judge are habitually practicing the very same things [that you censure and denounce].

ROMANS 2:1

A HYPOCRITICAL HEART

Anyone who judges and condemns other people for doing the same things he does has to be deceived. Yet to some degree, we all do that. We tend to look at ourselves through rose-colored glasses while looking at everyone else through a magnifying glass. We excuse our wrong behavior, while claiming that others who do the same things we do are deserving of judgment.

That kind of attitude is hypocritical and the same as the scribes and Pharisees of Jesus' day. Jesus noted that they put on a big show of being holy while refusing to help anybody (Matthew 23:2–4). Proud and haughty, they did good works only to be seen by the crowds and to be thought of as great and important.

All of that kind of fleshly glory means nothing to God. He is looking for people with a right heart so He can bless us. Our degree of spiritual maturity is not measured by how much we read the Bible or accomplish, but by how much we promptly obey God's Word and by how we treat other people.

✿

If there is pride in our lives, God is obligated to show us our flaws. He does not do it to embarrass us or to make us feel bad about ourselves, but to keep us in a place where we are dependent upon Him and merciful with other people who have faults.

GOD'S WORD FOR YOU

The heart knows its own bitterness, and no stranger shares its joy.

PROVERBS 14:10

For if you forgive people their trespasses [their reckless and willful sins, leaving them, letting them go, and giving up resentment], your heavenly Father will also forgive you.

MATTHEW 6:14

A BITTER, UNFORGIVING HEART

One of the most dangerous heart conditions we can have is unforgiveness. If we do not forgive others, we will not be forgiven, and our faith will not work. And everything that comes from God comes by faith. If our faith doesn't work, we are in serious trouble.

"But you don't know what was done to me," people always say to try to excuse their bitterness, resentment, and unforgiveness. Based on what the Bible says, it really doesn't matter how great their offense was. We serve a God Who is greater, and if we will handle the offense in the right way, He will bring justice and recompense.

Jesus taught us that we are to forgive those who hurt us, pray for those who despitefully use us, and bless those who curse us. That is hard. But there is something harder—being full of hatred, bitterness, and resentment. Don't spend your life hating someone who is probably out having a good time while you are all upset.

Never try to get people back for what they have done to you. Forgive them and leave them in God's hands.

Power in the Christian life comes from love, not from hatred, bitterness, and unforgiveness.

GOD'S WORD FOR YOU

When you go forth to battle against your enemies and see horses and chariots and an army greater than your own, do not be afraid of them, for the Lord your God, Who brought you out of the land of Egypt, is with you.

And when you come near to the battle, the priest shall approach and speak to the men,

And shall say to them, Hear, O Israel, you draw near this day to battle against your enemies. Let not your [minds and] hearts faint; fear not, and do not tremble or be terrified [and in dread] because of them.

For the Lord your God is He Who goes with you to fight for you against your enemies to save you.

DEUTERONOMY 20:1–4

 Faint Heart

Fainthearted people are people who give up easily. When the heart faints, it just gives up. It has to have everything a certain way or it quits. It gets discouraged and depressed quickly. The person gets his feelings hurt easily. Everything bothers him. He is touchy. In his heart he says, "I can't do this. It's just too hard."

In Proverbs 24:10 we are told, *If you faint in the day of adversity, your strength is small.* We can never stand against the enemy if we are fainthearted. And if we would enjoy the power of a positive mind, we cannot be wimpy or a quitter.

All of us have to resist against getting tired and giving up because we are being hassled by the devil. With God's strength, we don't have to faint, no matter what kind of adversity we are facing. The best way to fight the devil, especially in times of challenge and stress, is to just stay calm, to maintain a peaceful, gentle heart. Be constant, be fearless. That is a sign to the devil of his impending destruction.

And we must not be fainthearted with God's correction of our lives. When God is dealing with us, sometimes He has to do it over and over. Molding is never fun, but we will reap if we do not faint.

God's power is available to break a fainthearted spirit.

GOD'S WORD FOR YOU

Trust in the LORD with all your heart,
And lean not on your own understanding;
In all your ways acknowledge Him,
And He shall direct your paths.

PROVERBS 3:5–6 NKJV

A REASONING HEART

People who must reason out everything have a very hard time with faith because reasoning is not faith, and without faith it is impossible to please God.

I used to be a class A, chief reasoner. I had to have everything figured out. I had to have a plan if I was going to be positive. I was continually asking, "Why, God, why? When, God, when?" Then one day the Lord spoke to my heart and said, "As long as you continue to reason, you will never have discernment."

Discernment starts in the heart and moves up and enlightens the mind. As long as my mind was so busy reasoning apart from the Holy Spirit and contrary to the truth in the Word of God, Jesus could not get through to me. He wants us to use our mind to reason, but He wants us to reason in a way that lines up with His Word.

Balance is the key to victory in our minds. It is fine and necessary to make plans, but you cannot allow yourself to be controlled and manipulated by those plans. Say to the Lord, "You know the way, and I will be satisfied with that. When You are ready to show me, do so. Until then, I'll enjoy it and trust You."

If we try to figure out why everything happens in life, we will not have peace of mind and heart.

GOD'S WORD FOR YOU

For ye are yet carnal: for whereas there is among you envying, and strife, and divisions, are ye not carnal, and walk as men?

1 CORINTHIANS 3:3 KJV

An Envious Heart

Envy and jealousy cause us to strive after things that God will give us in His timing, if it is His will that we have them. A jealous, envious heart in no way blesses God, and the negativity spills out over others that He means to bless through our lives.

We need to be happy with what God has given us. We need to trust Him that if we are supposed to have more, He will give it to us when He knows we are able to handle it.

But you may feel that the devil is keeping you from being blessed. Look at it this way. If you are doing what God wants you to do, and your heart is right before Him, no man on earth or devil in hell can keep you from having what God wants you to have.

Many times, blaming everything on the devil is just an excuse not to grow up. It is an excuse not to develop personal character and let God do the work on the inside of us that He wants to do. Instead of focusing on the works of the enemy, we need to keep our eyes on God and let Him have His way in our lives.

God has a tailor-made, personalized plan for our lives. The key to happiness and fulfillment is trusting God to perform His good plan in our lives until we see results.

THE POWER
OF A RENEWED
HEART

*It is not the show we put on for others
on the outside that matters; it is the truth
inside us that we cannot hide from God.*

GOD'S WORD FOR YOU

*For the Lord sees not as man sees; for man looks on
the outward appearance, but the Lord looks on the heart.*

1 SAMUEL 16:7

four

THE POWER OF A RENEWED HEART

od is the God of hearts. He does not look only at the exterior of a person, or even the things a person does, and judge the individual by that criterion. Man judges after the flesh, but God judges by the heart.

It is possible to do good works and still have a wrong heart attitude. It is also possible to do some things wrong but still have a right heart on the inside. God is much more inclined to use a person with a good heart and a few problems than He is to use a person who seems to have it all together but who has a wicked heart.

It is very important that we get in touch with our inner life and our heart attitude, the way we feel and think about things, what the Bible calls the hidden man of the heart, if we want to have any success as a Christian.

When God seeks to promote,
He chooses a person after His own heart.

GOD'S WORD FOR YOU

And the Lord said to Moses,
Speak to the Israelites, that they take for Me an
offering. From every man who gives it willingly and
ungrudgingly with his heart you shall take My offering.

EXODUS 25:1–2

Let each one [give] as he has made up his own mind
and purposed in his heart, not reluctantly or sorrowfully
or under compulsion, for God loves (He takes pleasure in,
prizes above other things, and is unwilling to abandon or
to do without) a cheerful (joyous, "prompt to do it") giver
[whose heart is in his giving].

2 CORINTHIANS 9:7

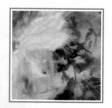

WILLING HEART

When we talk about a willing heart, we are basically talking about "want to." If there is something we want to do strongly enough, somehow we will find a way to do it. With it we can lose weight, keep our house clean, save money, get out of debt, or reach any other goal in life we may have set for ourselves. Our victory or defeat has a lot to do with our "want to."

We are really good at laying the blame for our failures on the devil, other people, the past, and on and on. But the truth is that most of the time the bottom line is we just don't have enough of the right kind of "want to."

God examines our heart attitude, and whatever we do for Him must be done willingly. God delights in those who give to Him willingly, joyfully, and cheerfully, but not those who give legalistically or under compulsion. I don't believe we receive any reward for doing things with a bad attitude.

We don't always feel like doing what we want to do, but it is not necessary that we feel like doing it, only that we want to do it.

GOD'S WORD FOR YOU

That is why I would remind you to stir up (rekindle the embers of, fan the flame of, and keep burning) the [gracious] gift of God, [the inner fire] that is in you by means of the laying on of my hands [with those of the elders at your ordination].

2 TIMOTHY 1:6

STIRRED HEART

God wants us to stay stirred up. It doesn't do any good to say, "I wish I felt that way." You have to decide to do something about the way you feel. If you want to have victory over your feelings strongly enough, you will do whatever it takes to get it.

How do we stay on fire? I have discovered that the Word of God coming out of my own mouth in the form of prayer, praise, preaching, or confessions is the best way that I can find to fan the fire. It stirs up the gift within, keeps the fire aflame, and prevents my spirit from sinking within me.

Passivity, procrastination, and laziness are the tools that Satan uses against God's people. A passive person waits to be moved by an outside force before taking action. We are to be motivated and led by the Holy Spirit within us, not by outside forces. The best way to guard against passivity is to do it with all your might.

Keep your God-given gift,
that fire within you, stirred up.

GOD'S WORD FOR YOU

*And thou shalt speak unto all that are wise hearted,
whom I have filled with the spirit of wisdom.*

EXODUS 28:3 KJV

A WISE HEART

I am absolutely amazed by some of the stupid things we do. We wonder why we don't have the things in life we want, when all we have to do is watch how we act.

In the book of Haggai we see a group of people who did not like their circumstances at all. God's response to them was, "consider your ways and set your mind on what has come to you" (1:5). For eighteen years they had put off something God had shown them to do, and yet they could not understand why they were not prospering.

We must use wisdom in anything we do in life. It shows up in the way we talk, act, handle our money, meet our responsibilities, treat other people, keep our word, and in a thousand other ways. There are all kinds of ways we have to walk in wisdom, yet so many of God's people are totally stressed out because they are going in ninety-five different directions at once.

Without wisdom, we will never experience the power of being positive.

One of the greatest tragedies in this life is that so many of God's people are just not operating in wisdom.

GOD'S WORD FOR YOU

For the eyes of the LORD run to and fro throughout the whole earth, to shew himself strong in the behalf of them whose heart is perfect toward him.

2 CHRONICLES 16:9 KJV

 PERFECT HEART

What does it mean to have a perfect heart? It means to have a heartfelt desire to do right and to please God. A person who has a perfect heart truly loves God, though he himself may not be perfect. He may still have things in the flesh to deal with. His mouth may still get him into trouble. He may make mistakes or lose his temper. But when he does, he is quick to repent and make it right with God again. If he has offended someone else, he will humble himself and apologize.

When God looks into our lives, He doesn't look for somebody with a perfect performance but a terrible heart attitude. He looks for someone who may not have a perfect performance but who has a right attitude toward Him. If we have a perfect heart toward God, He counts us as perfect and works with us while we are trying to manifest that perfection.

Having a blameless heart will make a major difference in your life.

GOD'S WORD FOR YOU

And become useful and helpful and kind to one another, tenderhearted (compassionate, understanding, loving-hearted), forgiving one another [readily and freely], as God in Christ forgave you.

EPHESIANS 4:32

But the [Holy] Spirit distinctly and expressly declares that in latter times some will turn away from the faith, giving attention to deluding and seducing spirits and doctrines that demons teach,

Through the hypocrisy and pretensions of liars whose consciences are seared (cauterized) . . .

1 TIMOTHY 4:1–2

 TENDER HEART

Having a tender heart is equivalent to having a tender conscience, and tenderness of conscience is vital in our relationship with God. It is dangerous to become hard-hearted and to develop a seared conscience so that we can't really tell if we are doing anything wrong or not. The key is to learn to quickly repent whenever God convicts us of something, not make excuses.

When God shows you that you have done something wrong, just say, "You're right, Lord, I'm wrong. I have no excuse, so please forgive me and help me not to do it again."

It is amazing how much that will help us have a tender conscience toward God and a positive mind. But as soon as we try to reason things out and make excuses for our wrongs, we start getting a little callous on our conscience. It becomes just a little bit harder for us to feel than the time before.

If we have a willing, stirred-up, wise, perfect, and tender heart, the devil may as well get out of our way because nothing can stop us from being positive for God.

GOD'S WORD FOR YOU

*My heart is fixed, O God, my heart is steadfast and
confident! I will sing and make melody.*

PSALM 57:7

A STEADFAST HEART

To have a fixed heart means to have our mind made up so that we are not going to change it. If we are going to experience any kind of victory and be positive in our lives, we must be determined. If we are going to see the fulfillment of God's will, walk in or follow the leading of the Spirit, or accomplish anything worthwhile in this life, we must set our face like flint.

And we must understand that the devil is not going to roll out a red carpet for us just because we decide to get saved and serve God. He is going to oppose us at every turn.

The problem is that because of the mentality of our society, we are always looking for something easy. We've got to be determined to do the will of God, to stay positive and happy, and to walk in the peace of God. His will won't just happen in our life. We are partners with God, and we must do our part. Part of what we have to do is never give up!

Press on with "holy determination,"
and God's plan will be fulfilled in your life.

GOD'S WORD FOR YOU

Though a host encamp against me, my heart shall not fear; though war arise against me, [even then] in this will I be confident.

PSALM 27:3

 Confident Heart

Not only must our heart be fixed and steadfast, it must also be confident. I have discovered that staying confident is a key to being positive in my mind and overall life.

The devil is constantly trying to introduce thoughts into my head to make me lose my confidence. The mind is the battlefield, and the devil lies to everyone through wrong thinking. The one thing that he's trying to steal all the time is our confidence.

The devil doesn't want us to have confidence in prayer. He doesn't want us to believe we can hear from God. He discourages us concerning the call of God on our life. He wants us to go around feeling like a failure.

We need to confidently declare what the Word says about us, such as, "I am more than a conqueror through Jesus. I can do all things through Christ Who strengthens me. I am triumphant in every situation because God always causes me to triumph." We need to read the Word to the devil, saying, "Is that what you think? Well, just listen to this!"

We need to get up every morning
prepared to keep Satan under our feet.

GOD'S WORD FOR YOU

A merry heart does good, like medicine, but a broken spirit dries the bones.

PROVERBS 17:22 NKJV

The thief comes only in order to steal and kill and destroy. I came that they may have and enjoy life, and have it in abundance (to the full, till it overflows).

JOHN 10:10

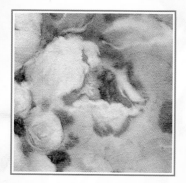

 A MERRY HEART

God is life, and every good thing He created is part of that life. We get so caught up in doing and accomplishing, in working and keeping our commitments, that if we are not careful, we will come to the end of our life and suddenly wake up and realize that we never really lived. God wants us to enjoy life and live it to the full, till it overflows.

We have a choice in life. We can grumble our way through our troubles, or we can sing our way through our troubles with a merry heart. Either way, we have to go through troubles, so why not take the joy of the Lord as our strength and be filled with energy and vitality.

In John 15 Jesus talks about abiding in Him. In verse 11 He says, "I have told you these things, that My joy and delight may be in you, and that your joy and gladness may be of full measure and complete and overflowing." Jesus wants us to have a merry heart. He wants us to put a smile on our face so everybody around us can feel happy and secure.

Don't spend your life waiting for things to change before you can become happy. Learn to be happy now.

THE POWER
OF A POSITIVE
HEART

God has given us a tool to keep ourselves
radically happy and peaceful.
All we have to do is believe.

GOD'S WORD FOR YOU

But without faith it is impossible to please and be satisfactory to Him. For whoever would come near to God must [necessarily] believe that God exists and that He is the rewarder of those who earnestly and diligently seek Him [out].

HEBREWS 11:6

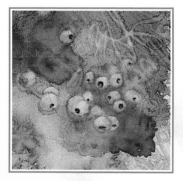

five

THE POWER OF A POSITIVE HEART

positive, believing heart is one of the heart attitudes that is absolutely vital in our relationship with God. That may sound funny, since we are called believers. Don't we all have a believing heart? No, we don't. The church is full of "unbelieving believers."

In Matthew 8:13, Jesus says that it shall be done for you as you have believed. It is amazing how much we can do if we believe we can do it. We need to get up and start every day by saying over and over, "I believe I can; I believe I can."

When the devil starts screaming in our ears that we can't get what we are believing God for, we need the heart and mind of Joshua and Caleb that says, "Let's go and take the Promised Land because we are well able to do so." We need to have the kind of believing heart that says, "What do You want me to do, Lord? Whatever it is, I'll do it!"

To live as God intends us to live, the first thing we need to do is truly believe that it is God's will for us to experience continual joy. Joy and peace are found in believing, and nowhere else.

GOD'S WORD FOR YOU

And I will give them one heart [a new heart] and I will put a new spirit within them; and I will take the stony [unnaturally hardened] heart out of their flesh, and will give them a heart of flesh [sensitive and responsive to the touch of their God].

EZEKIEL 11:19

A New Heart

The Bible says that we have to have a new heart. In Ezekiel 11 God promises to give His people a new heart to replace the stony, hardened heart that is in them. This new heart will be sensitive and responsive to Him.

This promise is repeated in Ezekiel 36:26 in which the Lord says, "A new heart will I give you and a new spirit will I put within you, and I will take away the stony heart out of your flesh and give you a heart of flesh."

Through the New Birth, or spiritual birth, we receive Jesus in our heart. It takes us out of the worldly way of living and places us "into Christ" and a new way of thinking, speaking, and acting. But even after that experience, we are told that we must have our minds completely renewed (Romans 12:1). In Ephesians 4:23 we read that we are to be constantly renewed in the spirit of our mind, having a fresh mental and spiritual attitude. Attitudes begin in the mind. Our mind is renewed by the Word of God.

We need an attitude adjustment every day,
and often many times during the day,
because it is so easy to develop a wrong attitude.

GOD'S WORD FOR YOU

My son, *if you will receive my words and treasure up my commandments within you,*

Making your ear attentive to skillful and godly Wisdom and inclining and directing your heart and mind to understanding [applying all your powers to the quest for it];

Yes, if you cry out for insight and raise your voice for understanding,

If you seek [Wisdom] as for silver and search for skillful and godly Wisdom as for hidden treasures,

Then you will understand the reverent and worshipful fear of the Lord and find the knowledge of [our omniscient] God.

PROVERBS 2:1–5

An Understanding Heart

I honestly believe that in the church today we are too selfish and self-centered. All of our thoughts are about ourselves. If we would think—really think— about others, we would be more inclined to do more positive things for them.

We need to seek understanding—to understand God's Word and will, to understand ourselves, and to understand other people. One reason we don't understand other people is that they are not like us. We think that if others are different from us, there must be something wrong with them.

An understanding heart is one of the positive heart conditions we must have. One way we understand what people are going through is by going through it ourselves. It is amazing how caring and compassionate we are when we have gone through a few problems of our own, and how flippant and judgmental we can be if we have not had the same problem ourselves.

We gain an understanding heart by seeking God.

GOD'S WORD FOR YOU

This is the [Lord's] purpose that is purposed upon the whole earth [regarded as conquered and put under tribute by Assyria]; and this is [His omnipotent] hand that is stretched out over all the nations.

For the Lord of hosts has purposed, and who can annul it? And His hand is stretched out, and who can turn it back?

ISAIAH 14:26–27

 A PURPOSED HEART

God is a God of purpose, and when He purposes something, it is going to come to pass. Jesus knew His purpose. He said that He came into the world that we might have life and that He might destroy the works of the devil (John 10:10; 1 John 3:8).

Too many Christians don't know their purpose and feel useless and worthless. God wants all of us to enjoy ourselves and to enjoy the life He has given us. But as far as our specific purpose, that varies from person to person and from one season of life to the next.

Whatever we do, we should do it purposefully. We don't love because we feel like it; we do it because we purpose to love others. So with giving, or being merciful, being kind, or walking in the Spirit. Love, joy, peace, patience, kindness, goodness, and all the other fruit of the Spirit are ours to enjoy and to release to others if we do it on purpose. We do these things, not because we always necessarily feel like it, but because it is what we are called to do.

If we want to be positive with our life, we must purpose to be positive because the devil will try to stop us a hundred times a day.

GOD'S WORD FOR YOU

But Mary was keeping within herself all these things (sayings), weighing and pondering them in her heart.

LUKE 2:19

 Pondering Heart

God does not want us to have a reasoning heart. He doesn't want us trying to figure out everything in life. But He does want us to ponder.

We can tell when we have moved from pondering to reasoning by the confusion we experience. If we are confused, then we are not pondering in our heart; we are reasoning in our mind.

Mary had some pretty serious things happen in her life. She was just a sweet, little girl who loved God when an angel of the Lord appeared to her and told her she was going to become the mother of the Son of God. But whatever Mary may have thought or felt, she controlled it because she said to the angel, "Let it be unto me according to the Word of God."

When God speaks something to us, many times we need to keep it to ourselves. If He tells us things we don't really understand, things that seem to make no sense, we need to do a little more pondering instead of running to others for advice. We need to zip our lip and ask God to make it clearer to our heart.

When God calls us to do something,
He also gives the faith to do it.

GOD'S WORD FOR YOU

Then Peter came up to Him and said, Lord, how many times may my brother sin against me and I forgive him and let it go? [As many as] up to seven times?

Jesus answered him, I tell you, not up to seven times, but seventy times seven!

MATTHEW 18:21–22

A Forgiving Heart

I don't know about you, but I am glad that God does not put a limit on how many times He will forgive us. We are willing to keep taking and taking forgiveness from God, but it is amazing how little we want to give forgiveness to others. We freely accept mercy, yet it is surprising how rigid, legalistic, and merciless we can be toward others. Yet the Lord tells us plainly that if we will not forgive others, then God will not forgive us.

The bottom line is, if we are going to get along with people and have a positive attitude in life, we are going to have to do a lot of forgiving. We hurt ourselves and make ourselves miserable when we harbor bitterness, resentment, and unforgiveness toward another person. It is exactly what the devil wants to get you bound up in.

We cannot be unforgiving and have the anointing and power of God on our lives. I cannot have strife in my relationships and still have God's positive power working in me.

God's ability helps us do things easily
that would otherwise be hard.

GOD'S WORD FOR YOU

One of those who listened to us was a woman named Lydia, from the city of Thyatira, a dealer in fabrics dyed in purple. She was [already] a worshiper of God, and the Lord opened her heart to pay attention to what was said by Paul.

ACTS 16:14

An Open Heart

Lydia was used to living under the Jewish Law, and Paul came to the city of Philippi delivering a message of grace. The reason an open heart is so important is that it allowed her to listen to this new and different message. It is amazing the things in the Bible we will refuse to believe because they are not part of what we have been taught in the past.

God wants us to be single-minded, not narrow-minded. We must have an open heart. It will tell us when what we are hearing is true. Our mind may be closed, but our heart must be open to God to allow Him to do new things in our life—not weird, off-the-wall things, but new things. Our hearts must always be open to the truth.

How often do we approach a teaching or a person with a bias or opinion, often without even realizing it. We have prejudices that have been placed in us by others through the things they have said to us. That's why we have to carefully examine our heart to see if it is open to the truth.

People who have wisdom are always willing to learn something new.

GOD'S WORD FOR YOU

But thank God, though you were once slaves of sin, you have become obedient with all your heart to the standard of teaching in which you were instructed and to which you were committed.

ROMANS 6:17

 An Obedient Heart

Paul wrote that the believers in Rome were obedient with all their heart. I have also discovered that it is possible to be obedient in behavior and not be obedient with the heart. It is not just a matter of putting on a show, but a matter of having the right attitude of heart.

I want to encourage you to come up higher in your obedience. Be quick to obey, radical in your obedience, extreme in your obedience. Don't be the kind of person God has to deal with for weeks just to get you to do the simplest little thing. Just do it!

We must be obedient to God whether we feel like it or not, and we must do it with a good attitude. Our obedience to God will ultimately always be rewarded. He is always trying to get us to sow the seed that is necessary to bring another blessing into our lives. We cannot outgive God; it is impossible.

A lifestyle of obedience to God brings rewards with it. The devil will give up when he sees you are not going to give in.

GOD'S WORD FOR YOU

Blessed are the pure in heart: for they shall see God.

MATTHEW 5:8 KJV

 PURE HEART

In Psalm 51:6, David tells us that having a pure heart means having truth in our inner being, which is the real person. It's all about paying attention to our thought life because out of it come our words, our emotions, our attitudes, and our motives.

Purity of heart is not a natural trait. It is something that must be worked on in most of us. In 1 John 3:3 we see that we should desire and work toward purity of heart because it is God's will.

There is a price to pay to have a pure heart, but there is also a reward. We don't have to be afraid to make the commitment to allow God to do a deep work in us. We may not always feel comfortable about the truths He will bring to us, but if we will take care of our part, God will take care of making sure that we are blessed.

God is an expert at removing worthless things out of us while retaining the valuable.

THE MIND OF CHRIST

*Believe what the Word says you are,
and that is what you will become.
Believe what the devil says you are,
and you will become that.
The choice is yours.*

GOD'S WORD FOR YOU

For who has known or understood the mind (the counsels and purposes) of the Lord so as to guide and instruct Him and give Him knowledge? But we have the mind of Christ (the Messiah) and do hold the thoughts (feelings and purposes) of His heart.

1 CORINTHIANS 2:16

six

THE MIND OF CHRIST

he Word of God teaches us that we have the mind of Christ. Consider what His mind was like when He lived on the earth, and then consider what your mind is like. If your mind wanders all over the place, if you get upset and confused, or if your mind is full of doubt and unbelief, you are not experiencing all that God desires for your life.

Let me remind you that the renewal of the mind is a process that requires time, and it's a process that Satan aggressively fights against. We have to purposely choose right thinking. When we feel the battle for our mind is too difficult, we must determine that we are going to make it. It is vitally important that we choose life-generating thoughts.

The renewing of the mind takes place little by little, so don't be discouraged if progress seems slow. Take a stand and say, "I will never give up! God is on my side. He loves me, and He is helping me!"

Our thoughts are silent words that only we and the Lord hear, but those words affect our inner man, our health, our joy, and our attitudes.

GOD'S WORD FOR YOU

Do two walk together except they make an appointment and have agreed?

AMOS 3:3

THINK POSITIVE THOUGHTS

If you are thinking according to the mind of Christ, your thoughts will be positive. Enough can never be said about the power of being positive. God is positive, and if you want to flow with Him, you must get on the same wavelength and begin to think positively. I am not talking about exercising mind control, but simply about being an all-around, positive person.

Have a positive outlook and attitude. Maintain positive thoughts and expectations. Engage in positive conversation. Notice that throughout His life Jesus endured tremendous difficulties, including personal attacks, and yet He remained ever positive. He always had an uplifting comment, an encouraging word. He always gave hope to those He came near.

Allow God to be the glory and lifter of your head (Psalm 3:3). He wants to lift everything: our hopes, our attitudes, our moods, our head, hands, and heart—our life. He is our divine Lifter!

Remember, you become what you think.
Change your thinking and be set free!

GOD'S WORD FOR YOU

You will guard him and keep him in perfect and constant peace whose mind [both its inclination and its character] is stayed on You, because he commits himself to You, leans on You, and hopes confidently in You.

ISAIAH 26:3

❧

As for me, I will continue beholding Your face in righteousness (rightness, justice, and right standing with You); I shall be fully satisfied, when I awake [to find myself] beholding Your form [and having sweet communion with You].

PSALM 17:15

❧

I will meditate also upon all Your works and consider all Your [mighty] deeds.

PSALM 77:12

❧

$\mathcal{B}$E GOD-MINDED

Jesus had a continual fellowship with His heavenly Father. It is impossible to have full fellowship with anyone without having your mind on that individual. The thoughts of a person functioning in the mind of Christ would be on God and on all His mighty works.

It is tremendously uplifting to think on the goodness of God and all the marvelous works of His hands. If you want to experience victory, you must make meditation a regular part of your thought life. Fellowshiping with God is the one sure way to begin enjoying life.

Jesus said that the Holy Spirit would bring us into close fellowship with Him (John 16:7). If we will fill our mind with the Lord, it will bring Him into our consciousness, and we will begin to enjoy a fellowship with Him that brings joy, peace, and victory to our everyday life.

Jesus is always with us, but we need to think on Him and be aware of His presence.

GOD'S WORD FOR YOU

And we know (understand, recognize, are conscious of, by observation and by experience) and believe (adhere to and put faith in and rely on) the love God cherishes for us. God is love, and he who dwells and continues in love dwells and continues in God, and God dwells and continues in him.

1 JOHN 4:16

BE GOD-LOVES-ME-MINDED

I have learned that the same thing is true of God's love that is true of His presence. If we never meditate on His love for us, we will not experience it.

Paul prayed in Ephesians 3 that the people would experience the love of God for themselves. The Bible says that He loves us. But how many of God's children still lack a revelation concerning His love?

First John 4:16 states that we should be conscious, actively aware of God's love. The love of God is meant to be a powerful force in our lives, one that will take us through even the most difficult trials into victory.

I became conscious of God's love for me through learning Scriptures about His love. I meditated on them and confessed them out of my mouth. I did this over and over for months, and all the time the revelation of His unconditional love for me was becoming more and more of a reality for me.

Let the love of God be strong in your weaknesses. God's love is the foundation upon which Christian living must stand.

GOD'S WORD FOR YOU

There is no fear in love; but perfect love casteth out fear.

1 JOHN 4:18 KJV

⁓

For our sake He made Christ [virtually] to be sin Who knew no sin, so that in and through Him we might become [endued with, viewed as being in, and examples of] the righteousness of God [what we ought to be, approved and acceptable and in right relationship with Him, by His goodness].

2 CORINTHIANS 5:21

⁓

BE RIGHTEOUSNESS-CONSCIOUS

Believers operating with the mind of Christ are not going to think about how terrible they are. They will have righteousness-based thoughts that come through meditating regularly on who they are "in Christ."

Yet a large number of believers are tormented by negative thoughts about how sinful they are, or how displeased God is with them because of all their weaknesses and failures. How much time is wasted living under guilt and condemnation?

Think about how you have been made the righteousness of God in Christ Jesus. Remember: Thoughts turn into actions. If you want to behave any better, you have to align your thinking with God's Word. Every time a negative, condemning thought comes to your mind, remind yourself that God loves you, and that you have been made righteous in Christ.

You are changing for the better all the time. Every day you're growing spiritually. God has a glorious plan for your life!

GOD'S WORD FOR YOU

He who exhorts (encourages), to his exhortation.

ROMANS 12:8

HAVE AN EXHORTATIVE MIND

The person with the mind of Christ thinks positive, uplifting, edifying thoughts about other people as well as about himself and his own circumstances. You never exhort anyone with your words if you have not first had kind thoughts about that individual. Remember that whatever is in your heart will come out of your mouth. Thoughts and words are containers or weapons for carrying creative or destructive power. Do some "love thinking" on purpose.

Send thoughts of love toward other people. Speak words of encouragement. Come alongside others and urge them to press forward in their spiritual life. Bring words that make others feel better and that encourage them to press on.

Everyone has enough problems already. We don't need to add to their troubles by tearing them down. We should build up one another in love (Ephesians 4:29). Love always believes the best of everyone (1 Corinthians 13:7).

We are not walking in the Word if our thoughts and words are opposite of what it says.

GOD'S WORD FOR YOU

Enter into His gates with thanksgiving and a thank offering and into His courts with praise! Be thankful and say so to Him, bless and affectionately praise His name!

PSALM 100:4

Through Him, therefore, let us constantly and at all times offer up to God a sacrifice of praise, which is the fruit of lips that thankfully acknowledge and confess and glorify His name.

HEBREWS 13:15

Develop a Thankful Mind

A person flowing in the mind of Christ will find his thoughts filled with praise and thanksgiving. A powerful life cannot be lived without thanksgiving. The Bible instructs us over and over in the principle of thanksgiving. It is a life principle.

Many doors are opened to the enemy through complaining. Some people are physically ill and live weak, powerless lives due to this disease called complaining that attacks the thoughts and conversations of people.

We are to offer thanksgiving at all times—in every situation, in all things—and by so doing enter into the victorious life where the devil cannot control us. It may require a sacrifice of praise or thanksgiving, but be a grateful person—one filled with gratitude not only toward God but also toward people. Expressing appreciation is not only good for the other person, but it is good for us, because it releases joy in us.

God delights in giving His children favor.
Offer thanksgiving to God, and as you do
you will find your heart filling with life and light.

GOD'S WORD FOR YOU

And you have not His word (His thought) living in your hearts, because you do not believe and adhere to and trust in and rely on Him Whom He has sent. [That is why you do not keep His message living in you, because you do not believe in the Messenger Whom He has sent.]

JOHN 5:38

BE WORD-MINDED

God's Word is His thoughts written down on paper for our study and consideration. His Word is how He thinks about every situation and subject. Anyone who wants to experience all the good results of believing must allow His Word to be a living message in their heart. This is accomplished by meditating on the Word of God. This is how His thoughts become our thoughts—the only way to develop the mind of Christ in us.

Joshua 1:8 tells us plainly that we will never put the Word into practice physically if we don't first practice it mentally. Meditating on (attending to, pondering, thinking about) the Word of God even has the power to affect our physical body. Proverbs 4:20–22 tells us that the words of the Lord are a source of health and healing to the flesh.

Remember the principle of sowing and reaping. The greater the amount of time you and I personally put into thinking about and studying the Word, the more we will get out of it. The Lord reveals His secrets to those who are diligent about the Word.

Words are seeds. What we speak we sow, and what we sow, we reap!

GOD'S WORD FOR YOU

Now the mind of the flesh [which is sense and reason without the Holy Spirit] is death [death that comprises all the miseries arising from sin, both here and hereafter]. But the mind of the [Holy] Spirit is life and [soul] peace [both now and forever].

ROMANS 8:6

For the rest, brethren, whatever is true, whatever is worthy of reverence and is honorable and seemly, whatever is just, whatever is pure, whatever is lovely and lovable, whatever is kind and winsome and gracious, if there is any virtue and excellence, if there is anything worthy of praise, think on and weigh and take account of these things [fix your minds on them].

PHILIPPIANS 4:8

Always Choose Life!

The condition of your mind should be as described by Paul in Philippians 4:8. You have the mind of Christ, so begin to use it. If He wouldn't think it, you shouldn't think it either.

Think about what you are thinking about. Satan usually deceives people into thinking that the source of their misery or trouble is something other than what it really is. It is by this continual "watching over" your thoughts that you begin to take every thought captive unto the obedience of Jesus Christ (2 Corinthians 10:5).

The Holy Spirit is quick to remind you if your mind is beginning to take you in a negative direction. If you continue, then the decision becomes yours. Will you flow in the mind of the flesh or in the mind of the Spirit? One leads to death, the other to life. The choice is yours.

Choose life!

A person will get out of the Word
what he is willing to put into it.

JOYCE MEYER

Joyce Meyer has been teaching the Word of God since 1976 and in full-time ministry since 1980. She is the bestselling author of more than fifty inspirational books, including *How to Hear from God*, *Knowing God Intimately*, and *Battlefield of the Mind*. She has also released thousands of teaching cassettes and a complete video library. Joyce's *Enjoying Everyday Life* radio and television programs are broadcast around the world, and she travels extensively conducting conferences. Joyce and her husband, Dave, are the parents of four grown children and make their home in St. Louis, Missouri.

Additional copies of this book are available from your local bookstore.

If this book has changed your life, we would like to hear from you.

Please write us at:

Joyce Meyer Ministries
P.O. Box 655 • Fenton, MO 63026

or call: (636) 349-0303

Internet Address: www.joycemeyer.org

In Canada, write: Joyce Meyer Ministries Canada, Inc.
Lambeth Box 1300 • London, ON N6P 1T5

or call: (636) 349-0303

In Australia, write: Joyce Meyer Ministries—Australia
Locked Bag 77 • Mansfield Delivery Centre
Queensland 4122

or call: (07) 3349 1200

In England, write: Joyce Meyer Ministries
P.O. Box 1549 • Windsor • SL4 1GT

or call: 01753 831102